ERIC WILLIAM GILMOUR

UNION

THE THIRSTING SOUL SATISFIED IN GOD

SONSHIP
INTERNATIONAL

CfaN CHRIST
FOR ALL NATIONS

Published by Christ for all Nations
Cfan.org
Orlando, FL

Sonship International is committed to inspiring a deeper awareness, consciousness, and experience of God's presence in the church.

E-mail: eric@sonship-international.org
Website: sonship-international.org
Twitter: sonshipintl
Facebook: ericgilmour

Printed in Colombia

ISBN 978-0-9898071-0-4

Cover design by Scott Howe
Evoke Concepts
www.evokeministries.com

Editing and Typesetting by Kathy Curtis
Christian Book Production Services
www.christianbookformat.com

DEDICATION

I dedicate this book to the eternal, immortal, and
invincible Godhead who has manifested His great mercy
throughout the universe by extending to mankind an
inclusion into His own gloriously blissful experiential
fellowship through the Gift of God,
the death and resurrection of the Son,
and the sweet presence of the Spirit. Precious God, You
are our salvation, joy, strength, and life.
You alone are worthy of all of our love.
I love You more than life itself.

THE SECRET OF HIS PRESENCE

In the secret of His presence,
how my soul delights to hide!
O, how precious are the lessons
which I learn at Jesus' side!
Earthly cares could never vex me,
neither trials lay me low;
For when Satan comes to tempt me,
to the "secret place" I go.

When my soul is faint and thirsty,
'neath the shadow of His wing
There is cool and pleasant shelter,
and a fresh and crystal spring;
And my Savior rests beside me
as we hold communion sweet;
If I tried, I could not utter
what He says when thus we meet.

Only this I know: I tell Him
all my doubts and griefs and fears;
O, how patiently He listens,
and my drooping soul He cheers!
Do you think He ne'er reproves me?
What a false friend He would be
If He never, never told me of the sins
which He must surely see!

Do you think that I could love Him
half so well, or as I ought,
If He did not tell me plainly
of each sinful word and thought?
No! He is so very faithful,
and that makes me trust Him more;
For I know that He does love me,
tho' He wounds me very sore.

Would you like to know the sweetness
of the secret of the Lord?
Go and hide beneath His shadow;
this shall then be your reward:
And whene'er you leave the silence
of that happy meeting place
You must mind and bear the image
of your Master in your face.

You will surely lose the blessing
and the fullness of your joy
If you let dark clouds distress you
and your inward peace destroy;
You may always be abiding,
if you will, at Jesus' side;
In the secret of His presence
you may every moment hide.

—Ellen L. Gorch, *Woman's Work for Woman
Vol. 12*, (Woman's Foreign Missionary Society
of the Presbyterian Church, 1882) page 389.

TABLE OF CONTENTS

TABLE OF CONTENTS

PREFACE

The secret to the spiritual life is a life devoted unto the Lord Jesus Christ. It is a life that is spent gazing upon the beauty of Jesus Christ. It is a life that is spent absorbed into the presence of God where the divine transaction takes place and the electricity of God so changes a man's composition that he looks, acts, and speaks like Jesus Christ, the Lord Himself. When the Spirit of God possesses a man, a man can reveal God in full manifest glory and power in the earth. And the dying, desperate need of a generation that is lost, sick, and diseased is that men would take upon them the mantle of the Holy Ghost and walk out in power and demonstrate, through the proclamation of the Gospel, through healing the sick and raising the dead, that Jesus Christ is alive, and that

He is coming back, and we must repent and put faith in the Gospel.

Lord, we need you. I pray that You would not leave us to our own ways but that You would keep us near You and near Your heart. Keep us in that place of first love. May we never graduate from the simplicity of the invitation to union with You. I pray that we would never deviate from the same road that You took, the same road that You are inviting us on; the narrow road. I pray that we would not just find the narrow road, but that we would also find the narrow road within the narrow road. That place where the only thing we can see is Your beautiful face. That place were we so identify with You as You so identified with us, so that we can truly come into that place of bridal union with You; that place of oneness. Protect us and preserve us by the cross. Make us objects of Your mercy, affection, and compassion. Fill us with Your Spirit. Fill us to overflowing, the Spirit without measure. Give us both the grace and the platform to reveal Your power to a lost and dying generation, condemned by the power of sin and under the power of darkness. Fill our hearts with the same love that You filled Your Son's heart with when He walked the earth. Fill our heart with the same love and compassion. Possess us with Your Spirit. Fill our hands with the same power, especially in light of these last days. Endue every single reader. Place dissatisfaction with living our lives below the means of what is available in and through the atonement of Jesus Christ and the release of His Spirit upon the earth. Even right now, I pray that You break the power of sin, disease, depression, self-consciousness, or whatever any reader might be bound to. As they turn to You, let the veils be removed. The Spirit of freedom unleash victory, Lord, my God. Reveal Your glory as seen in the face of Your Son, Jesus Christ, the Face of God. Bless us with Your presence. Fill us with Your glory and release us into a world to demonstrate the power, the love, and the truth of the Gospel, and point to Your return, in Jesus' name.

David Popovici
Founder of Kingdom Gospel Mission
Chicago, IL
Quote – Summer 2008
Prayer – Spring 2012

INTRODUCTION

In an attempt to set the stage for this book on union with God, I write this introduction on the light of His face. For that light is the very premise not only for this book, but also for the authentic Christian life. It is this experience of the "Living-Flowing-Light of the Godhead" that I believe is the nucleus of our redemption, purpose, and end. The Preeminent One is He who is the Word of Life and Light Himself—Jesus, God's brilliant Son unveiled by His magnificent Spirit. In common with our old friend, history, and our coming friend, future, today men must, in every way and at every point, be saved from themselves. Whether our eschatology would suggest digression or progression, it doesn't change the fact that Jesus, the Gospel of God Himself, is the only antidote to man's rebellious, destructive, and wicked heart.

"O Lord God of hosts, restore us; cause Your face to shine upon us, and we will be saved" (Psalm 80:3, 7, 19). Repetitive prayers are a rarity in the Scriptures and the objective of repetition is emphasis. This particular prayer is thrice in the eightieth psalm, penned by the burning heart of Asaph, the lingering adorer in God's holy temple. The people of God, the sheep of His pasture, are under extreme oppression. His repetitions prayer is a deep appeal for God to manifest Himself. And as God's heart for His people is inevitably infectious for seraphic gazers, Asaph is burdened to pray. The worshipping, praying, author of this psalm profoundly teaches us that intercession for man is the result of intimacy with God.

I wish to carve into your heart today this convicting truth: pleading for others comes from seeing God. Do you recall Moses' intercession for God's rebellious people occurring after his encounter with God on the mountain?[1] Think back upon Abraham's intercession for Lot; did it not follow his encounter with the Lord?[2] Let this

---

[1] Exodus 32
[2] Genesis 18

repetitive prayer in our current passage by the psalmist communicate to your soul the all-encompassing remedy for the rebellion in God's people

> **I wish to carve into your heart today this convicting truth: pleading for others comes from seeing God.**

and subsequent oppression on God's people. The paramount issue and direct medication to cure both the oppression upon God's people's lives and the rebellion in God's people's hearts is and will always be God's Radiant Face. [3]

Oh, the Chief Luminary! God has installed in creation an undeviating parallel to the brilliance of His countenance. The splendor of the suspended luminous sun shining from the firmament pictures for us the Resplendent Son of God shining in our hearts. It is a supportive analogy, yet as all types do, it falls short to communicate the whole, though we can hold it high enough to see through it a vision of God and His supernatural nature. No man has seen God, for He dwells in

---

[3] Psalm 31:16; 143:7

light that cannot be approached, the brightness of which is His very own person. For God is Light. In His mercy, and by His humble choosing, He has exactly represented Himself in the shining face of Jesus Christ, the crucified and risen God-man.

A right understanding of what is meant by the word "face" is imperative. For in the "face of Jesus" is the revelation of God. And within this prayer is a parallel between the sun that lights the earth's mountains, rivers, and fields, and the face of the Son who illuminates the soul by His Spirit. Without the sun the earth would be swallowed by darkness. Light is defined as, "that upon which all colors depend," simply because without its illuminative function, sight is inhibited. So it is with all things upon the earth and the earth itself. The sun is our illumination, the agent of sight in our world. The parallel is at no other point truer. Without Jesus, who is the "light of the world," there exists no vision, no understanding, no clarity, for darkness reigns with its fatal companions of confusion, doubt, death, and sin.

Asaph's intercessory prayer, in direct opposition to the oppression of doubt, confusion, death, and sin in the lives of God's people, is a prayer for the shining forth of the One and Only Face of God. Today we know that Jesus Christ is the face of God, "He is the sole expression of the glory of God, the Light-being, the out-raying or radiance of the divine, the perfect imprint *and* very image of God's nature."[4] The resplendence of Christ's face is the Spirit of God.

Perfect unity is in no place more clearly exemplified than in the Godhead Himself. Trinitarian intervention is the universal solution to all the dilemmas of life, both in the heavens and upon the earth. Asaph participates in the divine precipitation of prayer, requesting, without question in accordance with his personal revelation of God's person, the simple showing forth of God's person. The Face of God is the presence of God. God's presence is His Face. As the warmth of the sun upon the otherwise frozen planet causes life and productivity upon the

---

[4] Hebrews 1:3, *The Holy Bible: The Amplified Bible*. 1987. La Habra, CA: The Lockman Foundation.

earth, so the rays of the Spirit sent forth from the revelation of God in the Face of Jesus Christ is the origin of all vitality in our spiritual lives. It is Asaph's knowledge of this reality, undoubtedly through personal experience, that births this specific intercession.

> **Again, I say, intercession, born in intimacy, is inseparably united with our revelation of God.**

Again, I say, intercession, born in intimacy, is inseparably united with our revelation of God. Make no mistake about it, our revelation, and therefore our intercession, is bound up in our personal experience of God, which is and will always be through the shining Face of Jesus Christ sending the divine rays of the Spirit into our souls. The desired effects that Asaph is so confidently expecting from a direct contact with the Holy Resplendent Beams of the Spirit is summed up in the words "restore" and "saved." The Light of His countenance will, without fail, both restore and save.

Can we fathom that living outside of the reception of the rays of His Spirit, is a mode of living that we must be saved from? Is to live outside of the reception of His Spirit beams a living hell to us? Is it to us a prison of confusion? A sickly death? A terrifying ambiance? Or are we so familiar with sin's raping ways that we have lost all sense of the fact that His shining Face is our perpetual salvation? The reception of His Spirit is actual interactive fellowship.[5] And to know Him, the Light, is Life eternal.[6]

His presence is the illumination for our eyes to pass from confusion to clarity, from blindness to vision. He warms our souls with the sensible presence of His Spirit in the midst of the chilling winter of doubt. The reception of His rays into our souls alone makes for prolific lives. We are barren apart from His radiance. Dear reader, we need Jesus! We need Him today! Oh, the daily dependence upon the divine shaft of light cast over our lives! Such magnificence comes through the casting of

---

[5] See 1 John 1:7
[6] John 17:2-3

our lives upon Him. Such is the fountainhead of Life; the presenting of our lives for the reception of His life.

Divine fellowship is life for life. It was, it is, and it always will be. No matter the level of knowledge we obtain or positional revelation we receive or how flawless our track record, we will need Him no less at the end than we did at the start. I, you, we will always need Him. When I write "Him" I mean to say the reception of His radiant countenance shining upon us. Just as the light from the sun relentlessly lights up the earth and its direct touch upon our skin is an undeniable sensation, so is Jesus our illuminative God and blissful experience.

Jesus unveils one of the principles of the realms of God's glory saying, "I Am the Light of the world, He who follows Me shall not walk in darkness but will have the Light of Life."[7] That animating element of divine life glows with light. And inside the light of the Spirit is the life

---

[7] John 8:12

animation of the Spirit. We possess Life only in the Light and only in the Light is the Life of God our animation. Our vitality is wholly dependent upon fellowship with God, the light of His countenance. "If we walk in the Light...we have fellowship with one another."[8]

Have you a daily inward gaze sustained upon the glorious perpetual appearing of God in fellowship with His Spirit in the Face of Christ? Fellowship with Him is our sight and our pleasure; He who lights the way pleasures the soul. Such is following Jesus: fixing our gaze upon Him and then adjusting whatever must be adjusted to sustain our eyes on Him. Adam's transgression leveled the human race. His sin infected, without discrimination, all who came after him. Keeping in accordance with our spiritual allegory,

> **Apart from God's divine illuminative person, man is downward spiraling away from God.**

Adam's sin cast humanity from the Light of God's Face and the animating Life of the same. Apart from God's

---

[8] 1 John 1:7

divine illuminative person, man is downward spiraling away from God.[9] Hence, the deep burdened cry from our beloved lover of the presence of God for the "restoration" of God's people.

To what condition are we restored? Paul, the apostolic mastermind, trumpets the same depth of our plummet and the same heights of our aim, "All have sinned and fallen short of the glory of God."[10] You were made to exist in the glory of God no less than a fish was made to exist in water. Adam's sin removed all of mankind from the water. Everyone is dying. Our sins are every fighting movement of the fish without the ease of our God-ordained environment. But thanks be unto God, for by the beauty of His cross, the splendid spectacle leaking blood from nearly every part of His humble human body, we are restored to glory. We are saved from the fighting acts of lifelessness outside of that glory.

---

[9] Psalm 18:28
[10] Romans 3:23

The glory of God is the shining countenance of God in the face of Christ, radiant with the splendor of the Spirit. Our restoration is unto the luminous brilliance of interactive fellowship with the Godhead. He is the triumphant bliss, joy, and pleasure of life. The heat of the sun illuminates the barren earth into fertility, and God's Son shines down with the restoration and salvation of His

> **God is light.**
> **He passes through**
> **the unobstructed**
> **soul into the affairs**
> **of men.**

countenance, illuminating the human soul, passing it into Godlikeness. God is light. He passes through the unobstructed soul into the affairs of men.

I recently heard a story of a little Catholic girl who loved to turn her attention every Sunday to the massive stained glass windows of the saints in the cathedral during her Sunday school classes. The instructor one day submitted a question to the young group of Catholic pupils. She asked, "Does anyone know what a saint is?" All the children began to look around at each other without a clue as to what a saint actually is. Then the little admirer of the stained glass windows very simply stated, while staring right into a stained glass icon of St. Francis, "They are the ones that the sun shines through." Though the answer was so simple, even too simple, the simplicity of such an answer was the golden truth. It was the simplistic articulation and imagery of God's unification with man; we are those through whom the light of the Son of God shines. God is light, and if we live in the light of unobstructed fellowship with Him, He will shine through us in sweet union of Spirit, fellowship, and life. In the course of this book, we will explore this wonderful journey of the soul's union with God.

CHAPTER ONE

THE THIRST OF THE SOUL

"O God, You are my God; I shall seek You earnestly;
My soul thirsts for You, my flesh yearns for You,
In a dry and weary land where there is no water.
Thus I have seen You in the sanctuary,
To see Your power and Your glory.
Because Your loving-kindness is better than life,
My lips will praise You.
So I will bless You as long as I live;
I will lift up my hands in Your name."
—Psalm 63:1-4

It is not an uncommon line of thought that the soul consists of the mind, emotions, and will. Some suppose that this core of our existence consists of more than just the thinking, feelings, and will of a man, including other faculties such as the intuition and the conscience. Whatever persuasion has settled in your heart, I humbly ask you to allow me to erect a structure of thought upon which I may submit to you the word of the Lord concerning the thirsting of the human soul for God.

> **If one is to be conformed to the image of Jesus Christ, he must, by his will, choose to submit his life to the control of the Spirit of Jesus Christ.**

If you will allow me to unfold what the soul is through what may seem to be an oversimplification, it will be a great aid in explicating the yearning of the human soul for the Divine. Herein lies the structure I have chosen to promote in your mind the details of the thirsting human soul. The soul is our center and the center of our soul is our will. Man's individuality, uniqueness, and distinction flowers from his decisions. What one chooses is the path to what he becomes. If one is to be conformed to the image of Jesus Christ, he must, by his will, choose to submit his life to the control of the Spirit of Jesus Christ. Obedience is the yielding of the will to God. Disobedience is the stubbornness of the will against God.

Needless to say, the objective of the Spirit of God and the Spirit of the disobedience is to gain the consent of the center of man's soul, namely, that governing faculty designated *the will*. For all of our lives are displayed upon this platform of choice, both fashioning what we shall become and positioning our allegiance, either to God's Kingdom or selfishness united with evil. All influence upon the mind is with the intent to bend the will into agreement. In like manner all the influence upon the emotions is with the intent to bend the will into agreement. The soul at its core is the will of man implanted as the foundation under the mind and the emotions residing in a human body.

MY SOUL THIRSTS FOR YOU

The richness of our text is unfolding that the human soul is not only desiring God, but is also greatly in need of God. The will of man was made to be carried by the gusts of God's Spirit in concert with His divine activity. Simply stated, the will of man was made by God, to function in God, in direct accordance with the will of God. The soul was made to yield into a complete union with the triunity of the Godhead. The soul flourishes in no other place. Outside of this submission to the Spirit the soul decays, for it remains in the Adamic rebellion against God and His rule. The unredeemed man is corrupt unsubmitted to the divine will. The life of the redeemed is utterly dependent upon abiding in submission to the divine will.

> **The will of man was made to be carried by the gusts of God's Spirit in concert with His divine activity.**

To the degree that we submit our will to Him, our redeemed Spirit, one with God's Spirit, will take dominion.[11] As redeemed individuals, our repentance was not a one-time decision to submit to God's will and Spirit, but a decision to always decide to submit to God's will

---

[11] 1 Corinthians 6:17

and Spirit. Degeneration in a man's spiritual life is the result of a man's soul operating in independence from the divine infusion of God's Spirit, the very will of God; hence the internal awareness of the soul's deep depriva- tion. The soul thirsts for God.

This God-implanted composition inside of us all is alive only in submission to God's Spirit. Apart from submission to God's Spirit the soul is a fountain of wick- edness, restive, rebellious, and unmanageable, crying out in desperate thirst for satisfaction. Endless attempts are constantly being made amongst humanity to excel and attain heights and depths to satisfy what the mind thirsts for. And what many fail to realize through their whole sojourning upon the earth is that satisfaction for the soul apart from submission to God is simply not possible. Relationships and romantic ideas of life are tirelessly pursued in an attempt to quench the burning thirst inside of man's affections. But it is simply not possible. The man after God's own heart states, "My soul thirsts for You." The recognition in his spiritual life is that only the person of God, namely, His presence and voice, can extinguish the flickering crazed scramble of the soul.

Beloved, we need God. We will always need Him. He is the infinite pursuit. The endless wellspring of life. The unceasing source. He is the constant bliss, joy, and peace of being. Without His presence the soul extends itself toward other things, lesser things, things that can never satisfy, and if they are tolerated, they will inflict great damage.

I WILL SEEK YOU

Worship is the soul's attempt to quench its thirst. One can worship anything, for we are able to set our inward gaze upon whatever we wish. This is our individuality, the freedom to choose Him or not choose Him, which is the game of love. Oh, how He longs for our love. Though many profess God in the public place, God is only worshipped and adored truly by those who seek Him in the private place. Our musician, full of the rich, tangible presence of God, says, "You are my God; earnestly I will seek You."

To seek God is to intentionally set our will upon Him. God is only our God when He is our pursuit. To not seek Him is to reject Him as God. To not seek Him is to seek something else. The resolution to set the inward gaze of our soul upon God in earnestness and sober diligence is the only true worship of God. Frankly stated, God is only our God if we seek Him. If we do not seek Him, we are seeking something else. What does it mean to seek

God is only our God if we seek Him.

Him? It means that His presence, His person, His voice, His will is our one source life, objective of life, and ministry of life. In a thorough study of Psalm 14 we can see that when an individual refuses to take refuge in God, he states within his heart, "there is no God."

Oh, to keep before us the simple truth that His will is in His presence and His presence is in His will! Such a submission to God is entrance into a glorious experience of God. An experience in which is not only satisfaction but also rapturous delight that can even overflow in the soul to such a degree that the physical body can, at times, be pleasured. David states, "my flesh yearns for You." Have you had such an experience? The bliss of His presence so overwhelming that your physical body feels great delight? Such wondrous heavenly glories, regardless of the tribulations of life, are our lot. The bliss of drugs, sex, and pleasures in this world that turn men out of their minds are so far inferior to the ecstasy that comes from God. They are all counterfeits of the glory of God's person satisfying the soul through direct contact with Him.

> **In order for us to broker heaven into earth we must first live in heaven ourselves.**

This is our newness of life. God. God's presence is our newness of life. In order for us to broker heaven into earth we must first live in heaven ourselves. To live a life satisfied, blessed and in bliss with Him, is to be the representation of the salvation that we offer to the world. Anyone can tell me it is raining outside, but a man drenched with water as he walks into a room is dripping with the substance of his testimony. We don't want to merely be message bringers but message bearers. God is far more interested in making us into something than He is in getting us to do something.

WORTHLESS WORLD

The psalmist says, "My soul thirsts for You, my body longs for you, in a dry and weary land where there is no water." All things outside of God are this world, its system of selfishness and pride. All that the world is in itself is "dry and weary." May our spiritual eyes open to see that all this world has to give is bone dry with dust sweeping up, catching the wind, and settling again upon its desiccated earth. There is "no water" here, no sustaining substance. The world itself, with all of its glamour and charm, is totally incapable of quenching our thirst. We cannot be the extinguishing of the world's burning thirst until we, ourselves, are quenched deep within by choosing to "drink our fill from the abundance of His house."[12] Someone once asked me, "What is the world?"; to which I felt inspired to answer, "The world is every

---

[12] See Psalm 36

feeble delight seeking to take the place of the Highest Delight, which is God, Himself."

So many Christians are "dry," having not an ounce of bliss in their life. The reason is because they have sought for something other than God to quench their thirst. Even things about God take the place of God and the result is still the same, "dryness" in their speech issuing from dryness in their hearts. None of God's gifts can save us; only He, Himself. This is not only true for the sinner, but also for the sustaining of the saint. Only Him, forever, that is the Christian life. His presence is our life. Many are "weary" not just in ministry but in day-to-day living. They are tired and lacking vitality. They are spiritually sluggish and slothful, simply because without the satisfaction that comes from God's presence and person, found by seeking Him, they have directed their pursuits amiss and consequently miss direct contact with God.

They have replaced God with something else. They have replaced Him with something that allows the self-life to remain alive. They have tolerated something that gives a small measure of religious satisfaction, yet stopping short of surrendering the whole of themselves upon the altar. This is called idolatry, when we don't give all to God for the sake of keeping something else.[13] We must understand that the retained something is not living; it is lifeless, and as the psalmist says else-where, "They that make idols will become like them."[14] The idols have no breath, they have no voice, they don't eat or see—they are utterly lifeless, and if we choose to unite ourselves with them in any way, we will become as lifeless as they are. The lifeless makes lifeless, just as He who is Life makes alive.

> **This is called idolatry, when we don't give all to God for the sake of keeping something else.**

DIRECT EXPERIENCE OF GOD

Though the soul disunited with God endlessly craves God and the soul united with God is satisfied and ecstatically enraptured yet continually aches for the same,

---

[13] Remember Acts chapter 5, presenting part as the whole is fatal.

[14] Psalm 135:15-18

David, in our selected passage, speaks of a memory, "I have seen You in the sanctuary." He is recalling a past encounter with God that has whetted his appetite for more. Notice his reminiscent encounter is a vision in the presence of God (sanctuary). The beatific vision is that experience of God's sweet presence as he follows this vision with an explanation, "to see Your power and Your glory." He expounds on the beatific vision with two descriptive words concerning the encounter, "power and glory."

The power of God is the movement of His hands, His works. The glory of God is the splendor of His face, His person. These are coupled together by the anointed singer as a wonderful magnetic beatific vision of God. The following statement consolidates the seeking of God, the thirst of the soul for God, and the experiential vision of His power and glory—"Your love is better than life." The love of God in this specific context is united with the experience of God. The love of God is, in this sequence, revealed to be the glory and power of God; the living water sought for by our souls.

Too often men have fashioned a concept of God's love for man based upon His incomparable act on our behalf alone. We must understand that His perfect sacrifice not only imparted a positional union with Him, but also the actual experience of union with Him.[15] His great love revealed in the splendid spectacle upon Calvary is experienced through the presence of the Spirit. The Master Builder, through the Roman letter, informed us that the Spirit pours out the love of God into our hearts.[16]

> **The Master Builder, through the Roman letter, informed us that the Spirit pours out the love of God into our hearts.**

RESULT OF EXPERIENCE

The son of Jesse, moved by the Spirit of God, also unveils to us the source of genuine praise. Because Your love, the experience of Your person, power, and glory in Your presence is better than anything that can be experienced in this life, "My lips will praise You." True praise

---

[15] Dr. Jeff Hubing talking about the hyper-grace movement and distorted identity issues in the church at the time of this writing, "We've become so positional that it is no longer personal."

[16] Romans 5:5

is the irruption of a heart delighted by God. Beloved, recollect with me upon the greatest joys of life, whether it be the most delectable spread, arrival to a fantasized destination, or the gift of the most anticipated present. Whatever it may be that has ever deeply thrilled the whole of your being, whether innocent or even malevolent, nothing can exhilarate the whole of your being like God, the One who made your soul for Himself.

The devotion of the soul is gained by pleasure in God. "As long as I live, I will bless You." The whole of the writer's life is dedicated to the honor and admiration of Him who is sought by the soul, the Living Water in the midst of the wilderness of this life. The effects in the soul exhilarated by God are devotion of life, praise of lips, and lastly, the works of the hands. The works of his life are surrendered at the feet of Joy, Himself. "I will lift up my hands in Your name."

CONCLUSION

Only those who, by the submission of their wills seek God as the sole source of the satisfaction of their souls, make God their God. For this world, its system of selfish life and self-centered carnal pleasures and prideful self-exaltations cannot satisfy because they are dry and weary. If you are dry (unsatisfied and unfulfilled) and weary (tired and weak) today even as you read this, simply turn your attention from yourself and your self-centered passions and look unto Jesus. If we will live a life sustaining that simple gaze upon Him, He will both author and finish our faith. The encounter with God in

He will both author and finish our faith.

vision, power, and glorious presence are all an ecstatic experience of His love that pales all the pleasures of this life, inspires a lifelong devotion to adoration of God with illuminated lips singing praise, and the works of our hands lifted in surrender to God.

CHAPTER TWO

THE SATISFACTION
OF THE SOUL

"My soul is satisfied as with marrow and fatness,
And my mouth offers praises with joyful lips.
When I remember You on my bed,
I meditate on You in the night watches,
For You have been my help,
And in the shadow of Your wings I sing for joy."
—Psalm 63:5-7

The endless frantic seizing and grasping in an attempt to satisfy our souls is brought to an end by simply coming unto Jesus. That is what seeking Jesus is, the perpetual drawing near to Him. Jesus says, "Come unto

Me...and I will give you rest."[17] The tense of the phrase implies a continual coming, "Keep on coming unto Me." And the promise will always remain, "and I will continually give you rest." The life of rest is a life of endlessly coming unto Jesus. This rest means a life free from both the religious scramble to gain acceptance and the compromised scatteredness of a divided heart. The antidote to the uneasy antsy soul is the ease and repose of Christ's presence.

> **The life of rest is a life of endlessly coming unto Jesus.**

The restless life is a life of failing to come and keep on coming unto Jesus. All the desires of our souls are fulfilled in Him and Him alone. This is the communication of Psalm 63; all the desires of my being, all the thirsts of my soul simply cannot be quenched by anything other than God Himself. God alone, His presence and voice fulfill my inward cravings. I cannot avoid their momentum, but I can set them upon Him who is the Fountain of Life. As long my soul's desires are not aimed at His presence and

---

[17] Matthew 11:28

person, not only will they fail to be fulfilled, but they will also inevitably seek out injurious counterfeits.

ONLY HIS PRESENCE

The psalmist says, "My soul is satisfied." I am fulfilled. Seeking to convey the fulfillment of His presence, one has stated, "Being with Him is to feel as if I have everything I have ever wanted, be everything I ever imagined, do everything I ever wanted to do, and arrive everywhere I have only dreamed of going." In one instant all is satisfied. He is not just the soul's satisfaction, but also the soul's internal contentment, enjoyment, and pleasure. This experience is so much deeper than physical senses— many want a physical sensation, and those come, but they are so far inferior to the sensational satisfaction and ineffable bliss in our innermost being. The soul is what we truly are, transcending the physical. So the satisfaction of our soul is incomparably of greater depth than the physical. The physical is actually only a surface touch.

I have heard people say that "there are many pleasurable things, but only God will satisfy." This argument is still too flimsy to convey the whole situation, because He is the exalted satisfaction and highest pleasure. He is not pleasure without satisfaction. Nor is He satisfaction without supreme pleasure. He is simultaneously the highest delight, pleasure, ecstasy, and inward fulfillment and complete satisfaction. Heaven is Jesus. For some reason we have thought that the heaven of heaven is a blissful location away from the earth accessed by death. And though the fullness of our redemption is coming out ahead, we have seemingly missed the fact that the heaven of heaven is Jesus.

THE SATISFIED LIFE

Let not a limp and indifferent attention be given to the effects in the God-satisfied soul. "My mouth shall offer praises with joyful lips." The tongue is truly the most honest representation of a man's inward condition. The flicker of praise from the tongue comes from the fire of Love in the heart. Praise again is brought forth as evidence that God has made well the inward sicknesses of the soul. Joy is the mother to praise and praise is the sound of joy. The joy-filled life issues from the God-filled heart. Oh brother, dragging your condemning switch behind as you weary on in life's depressing way, find the fruit of the presence of

> **The flicker of praise from the tongue comes from the fire of Love in the heart.**

God's Spirit in your life through the joy of letting God satisfy you with Himself.

The fullness of this pleasure again influences the mind, causing a deep recollection upon God, "When I remember you upon my bed...." He lies upon his bed in stillness, contemplating God.[18] He ceases from all activity and reclines upon his cot, meditating and communing with God, whose residence is in his heart. Even in the midst of the "night watches." When the darkness and shadows of death cover humanity and the twilight of evil has cast itself upon the earth, our exemplar, the pursuer and ravished soul, lies in restful, blissful recollection and contemplation of God. He recalls the divine aid. As he begins to yield his soul to the breeze of God's endless mercies, he recounts the eternal faithfulness of

---

[18] Psalm 4:4

the Sovereign Ruler throughout his erratic life, writing, "You have been my help."

JOY

Once more we are educated about the soul that has drunk deep from the River of His Delights. We learn supreme pleasure of His presence is our lot and inspiration. Joy-irrupting praise is wonderful evidence of a revelation of God, but for joy to explode into song is to fly over the heights of the cliffs of praise. "I sing for joy," his love inscribes. Music is the soul's attempt to communicate itself above the medium of language. It is the attempt to cause one to feel what is felt in the inward emotions beyond what can be described with adjectives.

> **The Holy Spirit dispenses into our being the very ineffable joys of heaven.**

How glad am I that David chose this phrase, "I sing for joy." "The joy unspeakable" written in the New Testament is a matching phrase from two distinctly different pens, yet one Author. The Holy Spirit dispenses into our being the very ineffable joys of heaven. Richard Rolle wrote in his accounts of the sweetness of God experienced in the submitted human soul caught up in love with God, "I think I will die of joy." Friends, this is the shadow of His wings; nearness enough for the sun of trial, persecution, and affliction to be obstructed. Resting in the divine shadow.[19]

The same shadow is experienced in the life of the love in Song of Songs as she takes great delight in eating an apple of sweet taste under the enormous tree of God's person, shading her from the weariness of life and devils. Have you experienced such ineffable joy? This is the presence of Jesus; the shelter, shade, and cool of the divine shadow. "In the presence of the Lord is fullness of joy and pleasure forevermore."[20] "There is at once for the soul an aspect of stability and possession, which is her participation in God, and an aspect of movement, which is the ever-infinite gap between what she possesses of God and what He is.... Spiritual life is thus an everlasting

---

[19] Song of Solomon 2:3; Psalm 57:1
[20] Psalm 16:11

transformation of the soul in Christ Jesus in the form of a growing ardour; thirst for God growing as satisfaction in Him increases, which is accompanied by a growing stability, the soul becoming simple, and fixed ever more firmly in God."[21]

---

[21] J. Danielou: *Platonisme et théologie mystique*, Paris, 1944, pp. 305-307.

CHAPTER THREE

THE CLINGING OF THE SOUL TO GOD

"My soul clings to You;
Your right hand upholds me."
—Psalm 63:8

O h, the clasping, the clinching, the gripping strain of the one who is inches from death. With all the energy and power that the human will can employ, a man clings to his saving element when his life is in jeopardy. Even amongst animal life, clinging is understood. Are you familiar with a cat's loathing of water? As if he would melt upon contact, he struggles to keep himself from it. It doesn't matter who it is that tries to cast him into a body of water, he will sink his claws into the depths of that individual, in a desperate attempt to remain apart from the water. As a matter of fact, the definition of the word "abide" is "the refusal to depart."

The cat seeks to abide, remain apart from the water, by refusing to depart from the individual. He becomes like living Velcro®, attached to save his life. Can the picture of clinging be more vivid in the mind than the last effort of human self-preservation or the paranoia of a clawed creature? I say, yes, even more still, the unification of a branch with a tree.

We abide by clinging and we cling to abide.

The oneness yet difference between the branch and the tree. The branch is the extension of the tree in which it abides and the tree is the source of the branch that abides in it. We abide by clinging and we cling to abide. The abiding life is the clinging life. The clinging life is the abiding life.

CLINGING AND ABIDING

The actual Greek word Jesus uses for "abide" in the fifteenth chapter of John is *meno*. Its particular meaning is, "to remain or abide." In reference to a place it means, "to wait, or not to leave; to be held, kept continually; to continue to be present." In reference to time it means, "to continue to be, to endure." In reference to a state or condition, it means, "to not become another or different." The context is life in the Vine by the abiding branches.

The Glorious Son of God informs us, "I am the true vine...." "I." The personal pronoun used to refer to Himself. The fundamental truth concerning relationships is that a relationship is between two or more persons. It sounds elementary, but we must note that there is no relationship between a person and a building. Nor is there a relationship between a person and a system, or a person and a teaching, doctrine, or practice. A relationship is between two persons. Jesus said, "I...." Not things about Him, but Him, Himself. The subject at hand is the Person JESUS CHRIST; the real, currently living individual.

The striking revelation rings in our souls when Jesus says, "...am...." This reveals that abiding in the Vine is a current thing. It has to do with right now. The fact that He is the vine is significant because He didn't say, "I will be the vine" or "I was the vine" but "I am the True Vine." In that moment in which He spoke, He was the vine. And because He is that vine, today, as He lives as sure as then, He is right now the vine.

Often it slips the notice of the reader that Jesus said that He is the "...True Vine...," which gives a great implication that there exists a false vine or many other false vines. Jesus, in this very moment as your eyes cross these words, is the real, the genuine, the significant, the glorious vine (source of life), and everything outside of Him is another vine.

> **...everything outside of Him is another vine.**

Whatever the vine or connection may be that is drawn from in any person's life, no matter how positive it is or religious it seems, there is only one True Vine, namely,

Jesus Himself. The Person. The living, existing, God-Man. It is imperative to note:

- Prayer is not the vine.
- The Bible is not the vine.
- The church is not the vine.
- Pastors are not the vine.
- Ministries are not the vine.

What Jesus is saying by calling Himself the "True Vine" is that everything else apart from Him is fictitious,

"His presence is in the present."

counterfeit, imaginary, simulated, pretended, or imperfect, defective, frail, uncertain. The Son alone is life. The only real source of life is the person of Jesus Christ drawn from at this very moment. You cannot draw from Christ at any other moment than the moment you are in. Right there where you sit, Jesus alone is the river of the divine life of God that can be and must be drawn from, now. If there is to be any production, growth, or vitality in our lives, we must cling to Him. Say this with me, "His presence is in the present." His leading is in this moment. Christ's image comes from Christ's presence and Christ's word abiding in us and us in Him. "Abide in Me, and I in you."

Abide: Remain, do not leave, continue to be present, keep continually in Me. David said in Psalm 16, verse 8, "I have set the Lord before me." The soul can set the Lord before itself. And when Jesus chooses to use the word "abide" and David uses the word "cling," they carry an inevitable implication that it is not an impossibility to depart. It suggests that it

We remain connected and He flows inside.

is possible to not continue, kept in Him. "Abide" is a command to remain connected, just as "cling" is a clinching to remain. The connection has a promised response: the sweet grace of reception and reception of empowering grace. We remain connected and He flows inside. If the branch is connected to the vine, then it can receive the sap for life. If the branch is not connected to the vine, then it cannot possibly receive life.

Remaining connected is absolute dependence upon Him. The whole of the branch's resolve is to depend wholly upon the flow of life in the vine. As Andrew Murray so perfectly stated, "Remember the one condition; habitual, unceasing, absolute dependence upon Him."[22] Our command from the Lord is not to bear forth fruit or to yield our own increase, but rather to stay connected to Him who is the source of Life. For the sap alone carries the nutrients and power for the branch's fruitfulness. The demand upon your life is nothing more than, "Cling to Me for life."

"As the branch cannot bear fruit of itself unless it abides in the vine, so neither can you unless you abide in Me. I am the vine, you are the branches; he who abides in Me and I in him, he bears much fruit, for apart from Me you can do nothing" (John 15:4-5). Many ministers and Christians lack vitality in their lives or ministries simply because they are drawing their life from some defective, imperfect, or uncertain thing; namely, anything

---

[22] Andrew Murray, *The State of the Church* (Bethany House Publishers).

outside of the living interaction with the Person of Christ Himself. If the branch is not bearing fruit or producing signs of life, it is because its reception is not divine life. It is receiving something else as its source. It is the "in Me" that brings about the "in you" and inevitably produces the "much fruit." The clinging life is the abiding life and the reproducing life.

My friends, I submit to you that clinging is the result of the soul being satisfied with God, because deeply woven into this satisfaction is the internal enlightenment of what God's presence has saved us from. It is unspoken, unaddressed, and frankly, only those who have experienced the longing for Him and the satisfaction of Him can know that the salvation which He gives is Himself. And that which He has saved us from is a life apart from Him. In addition, we

> **He has saved us from is a life apart from Him.**

see that the life apart from Him is a living hell after one has experienced the blissful union with God, the purpose of His creation. The individual who still longs for the world and looks for the loophole in Christianity to satisfy their selfish, fleshly, and sensual cravings has no revelation of what life is apart from Him by virtue of the lack of genuine satisfaction in His blissful reality.

THE MIND

When the psalmist writes, "My soul clings to you...," this is the final stage in our "spiritual itinerary," entwined in the sixty-third chapter of Psalms. As earlier explained, the soul consists of the mind, emotions, and will. All of these faculties are unique, yet knit together in distinct unity. The mind is an incredible faculty. Its reasoning and recording of things seen and heard influence the emotions and feelings. Both of these faculties together influence the direction and submission of the will, which is to say, the path of the man.

David is addressing the totality of all three of these functions. He is saying, "My mind remembers You. My thoughts drift toward You. My mental faculties are defiled without Your pure influence upon them. Your infusion into my mind is the renewal of my mind and beginning of all my submission to You. My mind clings to You, the Central Source of All Good. I inhale Your Word through the Scriptures. I meditate upon and enjoy the succulent nutrients of Your written words, and my mind is quickened to supernatural life. My mind is quicker, livelier, eternal, and complete. My mind clings to You. Without You my mind is dull, perverted, ill, frail, and anemic. My mind clings to You. Meditation upon Your person is the purpose of my mind's existence. All the capabilities of my mind were designated to me for this purpose of being united with Your life, love, and reality. My mind clings to You." Some people think that because we are busy our attention to God will suffer in some way, but the soul was made to do all things through staring at Jesus. The soul was made to perform all actions, no matter how mundane, unto the glory of God, this being possible in our lives, as children of God, only through an internal stillness and

> **Some people think that because we are busy our attention to God will suffer in some way, but the soul was made to do all things through staring at Jesus.**

unbroken adoration of God that brings an infusion of Life from the presence of the Spirit, causing all acts to flow into the soul from God and flow out of the soul in excellence, manifesting the glory of God in everything. Hence our individual participation in the Trinitarian fellowship through the blood of Jesus having rent the veil that separated man from the presence of God.

THE EMOTIONS

David is saying, "My emotions cling to You. Everything points my affections to You, and all of my affections are set upon You. You are both the object of my affections and the reason why I have affections. The idolatry of placing my affections upon anything other than You will ultimately destroy me. But the utmost joy and pleasure are wrapped up in the setting of my affections upon You." Once God has the affections of a man, He has that man. The intoxicated singled eye of love rests like a fairy tale spell upon the starry-eyed princess. As Shakespeare wrote concerning the insanity of love, "How weary, stale, flat, and unprofitable seem to me all the things of this world."[23] The questions quickly arise following the soul's deep satisfaction with God: Can there be any pleasure without Him? Is it possible to exist any longer without His presence?

It is true that God is so jealous over His lovers that He simply will not allow them to enjoy anything apart from Him. But His lovers are so jealous of Him that they simply *cannot* enjoy anything apart from Him. He has swallowed up their existence. He actually consumes all the details of our lives because He has become life to us through the gaining of all our affections. Why do I use the phrase, "jealous of Him"? I do not mean that we don't want anyone else to have Him but us, but rather we don't want to give ourselves to anything but Him.

For instance, today I took my children to the park, and as I observed the surroundings my mind recalled a quote from Joseph Mary Plunkett. He wrote, "His cross is every tree." As I turned all of my affections toward Him, quickly every pavilion became a picture of the refuge

---

[23] Hamlet

of His person. Every rock became His written words. Every leaf became the healing of the nations. The shade became the cool of His presence. Every ray of the sun became the warmth of His love. Every refreshing breeze became the sweet wind of His Spirit. Every bird was His promise to care for me. Every sweet fragrance was the ointment of His name. Every grain of sand became His thoughts toward me. The lake became the still waters from the Shepherd's psalm. The sound of the children's lips became praise perfected and His blood dripped from every rose.

As I stared into the pond I heard His whisper, "I will make you fishers of men." Every time my daughter softened my heart with her tender two-year-old voice, my prayer rose to Him, "Let my voice give this very emotion to Your heart." My affections are overtaken with the insanity of love. As He woos our souls to Himself, our affectionate love for Him bursts out of our eyes in tears. I heard Leonard Ravenhill once pray, "I pray...that we will have to pull the car to the side of the road because we cannot see through our tears."

David says, "My affections cling to You." Many times a man's emotions overtake his thoughts. Many times the affections trump the mind. The Song of Songs is clear to show us this wonderful, dominating, violent charity. *My affections cling to You.* The satisfied soul is knit to God. That soul has recognized that only God is worthy of the insanity of love, and to pass this love on to another is idolatry.

Teresa of Avila writes, "My soul suffers out of desire for You." She is expounding on Psalm 84:2, "My soul pines for You." "Pines" is an anguished, aching desire for your lover. When was the last time your heart ached for Jesus? Have you been up in the night with tears looking into His beauty? Have you pushed the plate away out of a lack of desire for food, overwhelmed with a desire for God? David says in the forty-second Psalm in verse 2, "My soul thirsts for God, for the living God: when shall I come and appear before God?" How often the psalmist pours out these loving obsessions with His God. "The nearness of God is my good."[24] "One thing have I desired

---

[24] Psalm 73:28

of the Lord and that will I
seek, to dwell in the house
of the Lord forever."[25] He is
preoccupied with God's
presence. To the degree we
are not preoccupied with

> **To the degree we are not preoccupied with God's presence we will be affected by our surroundings.**

God's presence we will be affected by our surroundings.
But if we live a life preoccupied with His presence we
become invincible.

THE WILL

Lastly David is saying, "My will clings to You. I choose
You. I will Your will." The clinging of the will to God is
the eclipsing of your own will and the union with the
divine will. Jesus said, "Not My will, but Yours be done."[26]
He forever revealed the prototype of loving God. "Not
My will." Jesus says, "If you love Me, You will keep My
commandments."[27] Where is He getting this? If the soul
is set upon God as the first commandment imperatively

[25] Psalm 27:4
[26] Luke 22:42
[27] John 14:15

states, "Love the Lord your God with all your...soul,"[28] then your will is married to His. His commands become our delight. "I delight to do Your will."[29]

> **God's chains of imprisonment are the bracelets of liberation.**

As earlier stated, the will is the center of the soul. Once the will is subjected to God, that man is God's man. God is free in that soul to plunge the depths and to soar the heights. David identifies the fact that his will is only free when it is bound to God. God's chains of imprisonment are the bracelets of liberation. My will clings to You. I will not remove my will from Your breast because You alone satisfy.

The intimate laying of our heads upon His breast is the inevitable hearing of His heart. To remove my will from Your loving rule is to undertake the heavy darkness on my own. Such darkness cannot be battled, for its very substance mutates our desires against God. The light of

---

[28] Deuteronomy 6:5
[29] Psalm 40:8

His presence is our only good. My will clings to You, for if it doesn't, it bends against You, it deviates from You, it distorts thoroughly even professing Your name. O God, my will clings to You and such is the whole of David's existence set upon God, following His satisfaction with God, "My soul (the whole of my being) clings to you." Padre Pio, a beloved wonder-working lover of Jesus from the past, once wrote a poem in which was a line that struck me deeply. He said:

> *"Stay with me, Lord, for it is necessary to have You present so that I do not forget You. You know how easily I abandon You.*
>
> *Stay with me, Lord, because I am weak, and I need Your strength, that I may not fall so often.*
>
> *Stay with me, Lord, for You are my life, and without You, I am without fervor.*
>
> *Stay with me, Lord, for You are my light, and without You, I am in darkness.*
>
> *Stay with me, Lord, to show me Your will.*
>
> *Stay with me, Lord, so that I hear Your voice and follow You.*

*Stay with me Lord, for I desire to love
You very much, and always be in
Your company.*

*Stay with me, Lord, if You wish me
to be faithful to You.*"[30]

In the midst of great spirituality and leadership amongst the body of Christ, this old priest revealed the secret to the inferno of love in his soul; dependency upon God.

YOU UPHOLD ME

Herein lies the secret to an upheld life: "My soul clings to You and Your right hand upholds me." As we cast the whole of ourselves upon Him, He is able to hold us up. God cannot uphold the soul that is not cast upon Him. To not cast ourselves upon Him is to reject His divine upholding. It is not efforts and strivings that I reference, but rather a wholehearted, trusting, faith-filled surrender of our lives upon the altar of God. It is

---

[30] Forgione, Francesco. Prayers of Padre Pio. http://padrepiodevotions.org/prayers-of-padre-pio/ © 2012 Padre Pio Devotions.

His hand that upholds. He is the "lifter of our heads."[31] It is God who makes men faithful. For the "fruit of the Spirit is...faithfulness."[32] "It is God who works in us both to will and to do for His good pleasure."[33] It is God who is able to "present us blameless in the last day."[34] He authors and finishes our faith.[35]

It takes God to love God. It takes God to want God. It takes God to serve God. It takes God to see God. Friends, we must say with the psalmist, "I cling to You and Your right hand upholds me." It is not my efforts, my resolutions, my righteous acts that uphold me. It is Your response to my personal recognition of my own incompetence. I cling to You and Your right hand upholds me.

CONCLUSION

Recognizing the thirst of the soul, seeking Him by simply turning our attention toward Him in humble

---

[31] Psalm 3:3
[32] Galatians 5:22
[33] Philippians 2:13
[34] Jude 1:24
[35] Hebrews 12:2

> **I pray that God would install in your being a thirst for Him beyond anything that you have up until this time experienced.**

adoration, here we find blissful pleasure and satisfaction in His presence and voice, producing a clinging life upheld by and abiding in God. This is the abider's spiritual itinerary. It is the progressive stages of union with God. It is the soul's absorbing into the Christ-wrought union with God. Beloved, if you receive anything from this treatise, I pray that God would install in your being a thirst for Him beyond anything that you have up until this time experienced. I pray that the pining and panting of the psalmist becomes the reality of your life. I pray that your heart aches for Him. I pray that your soul yearns for Him. I pray that your inner being anguishes for Him with a pleasing pain. That with childlike simplistic, loving insanity you would pursue Him and find the wondrous, ecstatic, blissful, rapturous delight that He in every moment is. Together, let us rest under His shadow and dwell in His light. Let us bathe in His caresses and in rapt joy kiss His feet in adoration. For He alone is worthy, true, just, pure, and Holy.

CHAPTER FOUR

UNION REFLECTIONS – EMBRACE

"His left hand is under my head.
His right hand embraces me."
—Song of Solomon 2:6, NASB

It is my opinion that the soul is so deeply and thoroughly corrupt that once we dare to plunge its depths to offer to the Lord, it becomes severely imperative to continuously abandon it to the Lord (even more so than before) or the darkness of such depths, now awakened, will poison and destroy us faster than we can realize. In other words, the deeper you go in, the more glorious yet dangerous. The deeper you go in, the more it becomes a necessity to remain in. For the one who seeks union with God, it is simply not enough to merely be around the cloud; there is a burning fire inside to go *into* the cloud.

> **His exhilarating voice is reserved for the one who will go in, not satisfied with merely being around His presence, but burning to be absorbed by Him.**

Multitudes stand outside and are content there. But the desperate lover wants to enter the cloud Himself. This lover is convinced and convicted of his deep need of the voice of God. As the psalmist said, "He spoke to them IN the cloud."[36] God did release His voice from the cloud and around the cloud, but the speaking that is in the cloud is a whole other kind of speaking. The presence around the cloud is wonderful, but it can be penetrated. The experience of His presence is deep, but it can be plunged deeper. His exhilarating voice is reserved for the one who will go in, not satisfied with

---

[36] Psalm 99:7

merely being around His presence, but burning to be absorbed by Him.

BECOMING A VOICE

Once I was in an airport in Seattle, and as I was waiting for my plane to arrive, I observed a plane just after takeoff enter into a cloud. It was absorbed up into the cloud and the sight of the plane was no more. Such is the swallowing of the natural life in the substance of God. The two distinctly different elements become nearly indistinguishable. The lesser is swallowed by the greater. It is difficult to tell where one ends and the other begins.

Madame Guyon in her commentary on Exodus wrote, "It is the property of God's speaking to absorb our own." God is calling us into the cloud to release His speaking into us; not just to inform us of His desires or educate us in a message, but rather to make us His voice by swallowing us in His own substance. Not just receiving His speaking, but becoming His speaking. Noticing the lives of the prophets, they became the oracle, the burden, the actual speaking of the prophet issued out of what the prophet was. When John the Baptist was asked who he was, he responded, "I AM A VOICE...." He was God's means of communication to the world. This is what God is after. This is a prophetic generation, a people swallowed by God's own substance.

As we penetrate the presence and the presence penetrates us, His holiness and purity permeate us. The inevitable work of God's nearness is God-likeness. He is Truth and True thoroughly. As the light of His presence exposes our sins (Psalm 90:8) we cast ourselves deeper upon and into Him, Who alone makes men holy. The presence of God has this incredible dichotomous work to it. He will make us holy in His very own presence. His presence is the workshop of holiness.

> **His presence is the workshop of holiness.**

BECOMING TRUE

St. Patrick of Ireland wrote, *"...the lying mouth kills the soul. The same Lord has said in the gospel, 'on that day of judgment men will have to give an explanation for every idle word which they have spoken' (Matthew 12:36). Therefore, I ought to worry exceedingly with fear and trembling the sentence for that day when none can escape or hide and all will have to give an account even of the smallest sins before the judgment seat of Christ"* (St. Patrick: His Confessions and Other Works [Catholic Book Publishing Corp., 2009], 13).

After that striking account from St. Patrick's confessions, I was alone in silence for afternoon prayer in a church called St. Peter and Paul on the fifteenth day of March, and as the presence of God came heavily upon me, I was in an instant extremely convicted of the lies I have implied by remaining silent, or lies of embellishments in storytelling, or exaggerations for excitement's sake, or simply not telling the whole truth. So I reached out to the Lord for forgiveness, and as I did I was granted humility for repentance. When I was repenting I had a confirmation of the Spirit by gold dust on my left hand. I felt in my heart to check the date. I remembered it was March 15. As I thought of what the significance could be, the Holy Spirit reminded me of 1 Timothy 3:15, *"...I tarry long, that thou mayest know how thou oughtest to behave thyself in the house of God, which is the church of the living God, the pillar and ground of the truth"* (KJV).

The church is the *"pillar and ground of TRUTH."* We must be true. Jesus is the Truth. The Spirit is called the Spirit of Truth. I remember Art Katz saying, *"Men seek truths, but God seeks to make us true.* The truth is the whole truth and nothing but the truth or it is not the truth at all." So I pray along with St. Alphonsus Ligouri, *"... nail my heart to Your feet, that it may ever remain there, to love You, and never leave You again. I love You more than myself; I repent of having offended You. Grant that I may love You always; and then do with me whatever You will."*[37]

We must always remember that apart from Him, we are fountains of wickedness. And that if we leave His embrace our face will turn against Him. Abiding is not just a good idea; if we don't abide we will end up being

---

[37] St. Alphonsus Liguori, *The Way of the Cross* (Charlotte, NC: TAN Publishers, 2009), 15.

burned.[38] However you
want to look at that, be it
hell, outer darkness,
destruction of a life...
regardless, it is not a good

His embrace is where He speaks. His embrace is what makes us like Him.

thing and is a harsh image spoken from the mouth of the
Christ for a reason. His embrace is where He speaks. His
embrace is what makes us like Him.

HIS EMBRACE

I was watching Fulton Sheen the other day on
YouTube. He quoted two statistics that I thought were
particularly interesting concerning touch in the human
life. Two rooms were full of babies that needed care. In
the first room, each of the babies was cared for by individual mothers. In the second room, each of the babies
was cared for by one nurse. Thirty-nine percent of the
children in the second room died and all the children
in the first room lived. Is there significant correlation
between life and touch? In the spiritual counterpart,
could it be that the lifelessness, for a vast part of the

---

[38] John 15:6

church today, is due to a lack of touch? Not human touch, but the touch of God. Is there death in the church because we have failed to point people to the touch of God's hand or the embrace of His arms? Have our theological views relegated God's embrace of the human soul to a symbol?

> **Could it be that a large part of our deep depravity in prayer is due to a lack of our souls receiving the embrace of God?**

The second particularly interesting statistic was that babies who have very little touch in their lives take longer to learn how to walk and speak. Again, in the spiritual counterpart, could it be that many Christians have a very difficult time maturing by reason of a lack of touch? Could it be that a large part of our deep depravity in prayer is due to a lack of our souls receiving the embrace of God?

The analogy is imperfect because God is not responsible for the lack of embrace. The fault falls on our unwillingness to fall into His arms. My personal belief is that without the embrace of God in our lives, we are quickly decaying. When I say, "touch of God" I mean His sweet embrace. I mean His holding. I mean His genuine tight clinching of our souls into His warm and tender chest. I mean, finding in Him our only refuge from life's pressures.

LET HIM HOLD YOU

The other day I saw my daughter crying in her room about something. I was deeply concerned, so I walked into the room and bent down to her level and sweetly asked her, "What is wrong, baby?" She began to tell me her pressing issue. She expounded on her disturbing problem and I picked her up and laid her head on my chest and I said, "Whenever you feel frustrated, sad, angry, confused or hurt or anything...you run straight to Daddy and I'll put your head on my chest and you can find rest. Forget about everything else and just know that I am here. I can help you. After you calm down. I can handle whatever it is." She didn't respond with anything but a deep sigh of comfort and quietness as she rested on my chest and I rubbed her back. In that moment, though there were no words going back and forth, we were communicating. I believe we were communicating higher than words. I believe we were exchanging. There was a transferring of my rest into her problem.

Brothers and sisters, the embrace of God is so important. Can you hear Him saying that to you? Can you see His beckoning hand? Can you imagine His open arms? Allow the Spirit of God to woo you away from your sins, failures, weaknesses, performance, strivings, issues, troubles, and trials, into His arms. This is simultaneously the mark of maturity and the maturing work; how well we remain in His embrace.

EMBRACE OF THE LOVER

Song of Songs 2:5-6 connects the lovesickness of the bride with the embrace of the lover. Lovesickness is defined as being so deeply affected by love as to be unable to act normally. It is to be so fixed upon the object of your affection that one's whole being is affected. The source of lovesickness is the embrace of God in Christ through the Spirit. The lovesickness of the soul is for the divine embrace of the Beloved.

We need a fresh embrace of God. We need a sweet, intimate experience of Jesus. We need a cooling drink of the Spirit. This direct contact with God through a surrendered, yielded, trusting faith is the embrace for which our souls are longing for. Though it may come through a meeting, a conference, a situation, a rock-bottom experience, it doesn't have to. It should be the source of our daily joy, life, peace, and strength. Nothing is more genuine and effective than when we, by our own will, choose to lay everything else aside and simply come to Him.

> **Nothing is more genuine and effective than when we, by our own will, choose to lay everything else aside and simply come to Him.**

HOW TO ENTER THE EMBRACE

Come to Him fresh today, with no agenda but to let Him hold you. Just sit in adoration of Him, casting all of yourself helplessly upon Him, and give attention to the sweet presence of the Spirit. Sustain it until the soul is washed over with the refreshing river of the Spirit and filled with the Love of the Father, and remain.

One of the first keys to experiencing intimacy with Jesus is the understanding that He is the man in the relationship and we are the women. We receive. The bride didn't say, "I am going to kiss him with the kisses of my mouth," but rather, "Let Him kiss me...." Yielding is the secret; the ceasing of efforts and our still surrender in adoration. Everything aside, He just wants your heart (mind, will, and emotions). When we come to Him, we do not come to intercede for others or gain answers to prayer or fulfill a religious duty. We don't come to Him to manipulate Him into doing something for us. We do not even come to Him because we need to. Though we do need to, it is not the motive.

Once God spoke to my heart and said, "If you seek Me for power, you will forfeit intimacy." We come simply because there is no greater lover or pleasure in the entire world and this is the reason why we were created by God—to live in God. We simply come to Him because we just want to be with Him. Only He is lovely, wonderful, and true. He is truly holy, meaning altogether separate and other than anything else. We must have a genuine desire to want to be with Him. Without this, or if this is trumped by anything else, no matter how noble or legitimate, we are bankrupt. *Please catch this.* We come to Him for no other reason than Him. Do you love His presence? Do you love His voice? In Mark chapter 3,

We come to Him for no other reason than Him.

His presence and voice were exactly what Jesus set the disciples aside for, *"To be with Him."*

THE EMBRACE OF A MOTHER

Again we see this embrace in Psalm 131. The Scripture says, *"I have...quieted my soul; like a weaned child rests upon His mother, my soul is like a weaned child...."* My mind, emotions, and will rest upon You, O God. There exists something indefinable and so indescribable that transpires when the child rests upon his mother. There is no word to explain it. But a picture is worth a thousand words, so the Scripture can only describe its situation. Oh, the child upon the breast of its mother. This is what will be experienced in the mind, will, and emotions of a man, when the soul is quieted and wholly leaning upon God.

If you are in turmoil in your mind, or tossed around by your emotions, in any given situation, or if your will is so wickedly bucking against the will of God, *shut the door and meet with your Father who is in secret.* The word "secret" there can mean, *"within."* God is within, by His Holy Spirit. Close the door on the noise of the world and simply come to Him and let Him hold you.

> **Just wordlessly rest upon His breast and you will gain access to the divine treasure chest.**

No words, complaints, or fervent religious exercises. Just wordlessly rest upon His breast and you will gain access to the divine treasure chest.

A weaned child is one that is old enough to run away, or make the decision to come to its mother when it wills. So the decision is yours to make. Come to Him and let Him hold you. When a child is tired, the only thing that they want is to be held. It is the only place they find contentment and peace. So many of you are so tired and worn out from life's ways and weights. Come to Him and let Him hold you—find peace and life and strength and grace and satisfaction in His arms alone. He is rest from the constant pressure of the soul's desire to perform and conger up. One of the greatest hindrances to the spiritual life is the soul's itch to make something happen. And all God is wanting is for someone to simply come to Him. "My soul, wait in silence for God only, for my hope is from Him. He only is my rock and my salvation, my stronghold; I shall not be shaken. On God my salvation and my glory rest; the rock of my strength, my refuge is in God. Trust in Him at all times, O people; pour out your heart before Him; God is a refuge for us."[39]

---

[39] Psalm 62:5-8

CHAPTER FIVE

UNION REFLECTIONS – REPOSE

*"For thus said the Lord God, the Holy One of Israel:
In returning [to Me] and resting [in Me] you shall
be saved; in quietness and in [trusting]
confidence shall be your strength."*
—Isaiah 30:15, AMP

The motorboat is engine driven and the sailboat progresses by the wind. The motorboat forces motion through its power while the sailboat drifts by its surrendered sails. I write this to encourage a life that surrenders its sails to the wind of the Spirit, so that the divine ease may be our mastery instead of the independent force and flash of human ingenuity, pressure, and performance.

God is at rest and the significance of entering into the divine repose is that man enters into the dwelling place of God. When man exits the rest, he exits the dwelling of God. It was Mary of the Holy Trinity who died in 1942 who said that God quickened her heart with these powerful words, *"Let Me act; you are not competent to do anything; it is not your province.... The most important work is not that which you do, it is that which you allow Me to do."*[40]

Madame Guyon noted in her book, *"Short and Easy Method of Prayer"* that, "Religion applies the remedy to the outward body while the disease lies at the heart."[41] That is why we must disciple men into the "prayer of the heart" rather than just the "prayer of understanding." She

[40] Father Bartholomew Gottemoller, *Word of Love: Revelations of Our Lord to Three Victim Souls in the 20th Century* (Rockford, IL: TAN Books and Publishers, Inc., 1985), 5.

[41] Madame Jeanne-Marie Bouvier de la Motte-Guyon, *"Short and Easy Method of Prayer"* (Shippensburg, PA: Destiny Image Publishers, Inc., 2007), 147.

states, "For all that is of man's own power or exertion must first die, be it ever so noble or exalted." Why? Because, "Nothing is so opposed to God as self-sufficiency." She writes, "Activity obstructs union, for God being in infinite stillness, the soul must participate in this stillness. Else the contrariety between stillness and activity would prevent assimilation; therefore the soul can never arrive at divine union without the repose of the will."

God is resting from all His works (Hebrews 4:4) and our only work is to diligently enter His rest; to align ourselves with what He has finished. Sin is independent soulical activity, when the soul acts of itself apart from the Spirit's quickening. But the rest of God infiltrating every facet of the soul will produce effortless God-likeness. The reason is because in this submissive disposition, it is God Himself who acts through the man and not the man for God. Rest is the submission of the soul to the Spirit's leading and empowerment. Jesus said,

> **God is not looking for people who will simply do the work, but those through whom He can work.**

"...My Father abiding in me does His works."[42] He also said, *"...I do nothing on my own initiative...."*[43] Those that are *"...led by the Spirit are the sons of God."*[44] This is the divine repose, that resting place where the works of God Himself become ours. God is not looking for people who will simply do the work, but those through whom He can work.

This is the simple sweetness of our God and Gospel:

"Repose each care of your load on Him; trust, lean on, rely on, and be confident also in Him and he will bring it to pass.... Be still and rest in the Lord; wait for Him and patiently lean yourself upon Him" (Psalm 37:4-7, AMP).

Julian of Norwich wrote:

"The reason we are not fully at rest in heart and soul is because we seek rest in those things that

---

[42] John 14:10
[43] John 8:28
[44] Romans 8:14

are so small and have no rest within them, and pay no attention to our God, who is Almighty, All-wise, All-good, and the only real rest."[45]

Mary of the Holy Trinity said that the Holy Spirit said similar words to her:

"To find Me, to know Me, to receive Me...come to Me—that is the only meaning of every life. All activities, all zeal are subordinate to coming to Me, and have only the value of means, in the measure in which they lead to Me. I am the Alpha and Omega, your God and your All. How is it, then, that in so many lives, I am accepted and treated merely as something supplementary?"[46]

Recently moved to tears by the mystical, miracle, and bridal love life of St. John of Vianney, otherwise known as

---

[45] As quoted by Sarah Gallick, *The Big Book of Women Saints* (New York, NY: Harper Collins, 2007), 145.

[46] Father Bartholomew Gottemoller, *Word of Love: Revelations of Our Lord to Three Victim Souls in the 20th Century* (Rockford, IL: TAN Books and Publishers, Inc., 1985).

the Cure' d'Ars, I broke inside as I was reading this sweet quote on prayer as resting in His embrace:

> *"Oh! the beautiful union of the soul with Our Lord! The interior life is a bath of love into which the soul plunges. God holds the soul, when she has reached that stage, as a mother embraces the head of her child in order to cover it with caresses. Our Lord hungers after such a soul."*[47]

He also writes concerning prayer, "...you need not say much to pray well...you feel something extraordinary, a feeling of well-being that runs through all your body and all you can say is, 'That is the Lord....'"

REST AND PRESENCE

Are we going to rest with Him or are we going to try to make something happen? That is the distinguishing factor. Force or flow. Response or repose. Restless or rest.

---

[47] St. John of Vianney, the Cure' d'Ars. Quoted by Joan Carroll Cruz, *Mysteries Marvels Miracles: In the Lives of the Saints* (Charlotte, NC: TAN Books and Publishers, 1997), 150.

Energy or ease. God gives rest in His presence. To live outside of rest is to live outside His presence. Those that don't rest are normally spent, tired, and burn out quickly. I remember one particular instance at work when my Christian boss lost his temper at me. I was questioning the validity of his salvation. Then the Holy Spirit spoke to my heart, "You would be just the same if you went as long as he has without resting in Me."

We become like hamsters running on a wheel of performance. But when we rest in Him we find fruitfulness in everything that we do, because God is the One who has worked. God revealed His glorious union with man when He spoke to Moses, "My presence shall go with you and I will give you rest..." (Exodus 33:14, AMP). Notice the link between His presence and His rest.

The rest was Moses' present possession both in the going to Egypt and the destination from Egypt, the "Land of Promise." The reason why He delivered the Children of Israel from the dominion, bondage, and slavery of Egypt was to bring them into the "Land of Promise," the sweet rest of God's rule, guidance, leading, provision, and power overflowing with milk and honey. He is a good Father and loves to take care of us.

Rest is the place of ceasing to act that He alone may act. It is defined in Webster's dictionary as, *"Refreshing ease—inactivity and freedom from weariness. Repose, tranquility, spiritual calm and cessation of motion."* The significance of the verb form is, *"refresh by relaxing to be at ease. To have tranquility or peace to become or remain inactive."*

> **When the soul rests in God, then the Spirit acts. When the soul acts on its own, the Spirit does not.**

When the soul rests in God, then the Spirit acts. When the soul acts on its own, the Spirit does not. Before I minister I pay close attention to my nerves because if I am nervous, I am not at rest. If I am not at rest, then I am working. If I am at rest, then God is working. The only way to be led is for the soul to enter rest. The only way to not be led is to act independently without rest in God. It is very simple. Let us stop pulling our hair out and just relax, enjoy Jesus, and stay behind the Holy Ghost. "The Spirit of the Lord gave them rest. So you led Your people."[48] The rest is a gift from the Spirit. The leading follows the gift of rest. The Spirit outside of rest leads no one. Rest is the platform for leading.

Worry, sin, unbelief, lusts, and selfishness are all products of not resting. They are the soul's tired acts. Sin, worry, and unbelief all flow out of the active soul. Rest will silence them and give you, faith, trust, and strength. Looking into Psalm 38, it is evident that rest is robbed by sin and sin is lack of rest.

Below is a prayer I copied from my journal:

"Being with You is sweet, restful bliss. With highs of spiritually erotic ecstasies surging through my soul. Hearing You in that sweet, restful still-ness is like unveiling mysteries that feed my

---

[48] Isaiah 63:14

soul with the richest of delightful foods. Your wine and honey—sever my soul from earthly pleasures."

MYSTICAL REPOSE

In the ocean of religious writing, there exists a company of spiritual masters enlightened through the indescribable experience of divine inebriation. It is as if He, the Chief Luminary, has reserved a unique unveiling of truth for those whose hearts are torched with ardent affection for Him. Those hidden spiritual realities are locked away in the vault of simplicity, in the realm of experiencing the glory of His presence. These rare individuals are called "Christian mystics"; those who seek oneness with God through surrender; those who enter knowledge of God, not by mere study, but by direct experience. The theologian, through study, retains in his intellect what the mystic is actually becoming, by experience. The motif of scholastic theology is, "We believe to understand." The motif in mystical theology is, "We believe to experience."

Inge writes:

Christian mysticism may be defined as the attempt to realize the presence of the living God in the soul. As Goethe says, "Mysticism is the scholastic of the heart, the dialect of the feelings."

The first principle of mysticism: The soul can see and perceive. We have an organ or faculty for the discernment of spiritual truth.

The second principle of mysticism: We can only know what is akin to ourselves. Man, in order to know God, must be a partaker of the divine nature. Ruusbroec writes, "What we are, that we behold: and what we behold, that we are." Though we are made in the image of God, our likeness to Him only exists potentially. The divine spark already shines within us, but it has to be searched out in the inmost depths of our person, and its light defused over our whole being.The third principle of mysticism: Sensuality and selfishness are absolute disqualification for knowing the things of the Spirit of God.[49]

One indispensable element of the mystical life—whether your eyes cross the golden literature of Madame Guyon, St. Teresa of Jesus, John Ruusbroec, Angelina of Foligno, John Tauler, Richard Rolle, Walter Hilton, Henry Suzo, St. John of the Cross, François Fénelon, Miguel de Molinos, Gregory of Nyssa, St. Gregory the Great, St. Augustine, Richard of St. Victor, John Cassian, Evagrius Ponticus, Dionysius, Julian of Norwich, St. Bridget of Sweden, Origen, Bernard of Clairvaux, Hadewijch, Mechtild of Magdeburg, or any other of these incredible lovesick seekers whose lives were wrapped up in the Divine, all of them share this spiritual element to be indispensible for deep contact and fellowship with the Holy Spirit. This indispensable element in prayer and living is called "repose." It is both the door and the platform for spiritual union.

---

[49] W. R. Inge, *Christian Mysticism* (London: Methuen & Co. LTD, 1899), 5, 6.

"Repose is the 'perfection' of activity...."[50] Repose is the rest of the soul. It is inactivity, stillness, and even a relaxation. Madam Guyon spoke of it as "mystical slumber." So the question arises, "How can repose be the perfection of activity when its very definition is inactivity?" It is because the ignition of divine activity is soulical inactivity. What does that mean? It is exactly what Jesus said was the prerequisite for following Him. He said in Matthew 16:24, "If any man would come after me (which is to follow) he must deny himself (his own soulical man or self-life)...."

You cannot in your own power follow Jesus. You must enter the inactivity of the soul in order to be infused with divine empowerment to be able to "pick up your cross." Man doesn't have the power to pick up the cross, but it will be granted to him if he will reject himself. That death (inactivity) will quicken divine enablement (resurrection—the infusion of God's power). This repose is the perfection of activity because it is the only route to God's

---

[50] Paul Mommaers, "Bulletin d'histoire de la spiritualité: L'Ecole néerlandaise," *Revue d'histoire de la Spiritualité* 49 (1973), 474.

activity through man. Jesus said, "I do nothing on My own initiative." And as earlier stated, "My Father abiding in Me does His works."

Dr. Robert Gladstone told us an amazing story of when he was in Wales during the last minutes of an old man of God's life. This man of God seized this young man of God and passed on to him a secret that he had learned through decades of faithfully walking with God.

The only thing that pleases God is what He does Himself.

He said, "The only thing that pleases God is what He does Himself." No wonder we "obey the truth by the Spirit." No wonder it is God's design that we "put to death the deeds of the flesh by the Spirit." It was T. Austin Sparks who said, "Only God can produce after His own kind."

Repose is the perfection of activity.

CHAPTER SIX

UNION IN COMMUNION

"...the fellowship of the Holy Spirit, be with you all."
—2 Corinthians 13:14, NASB

I don't think that anyone would say, "No, I do not want to experience God when I pray." So the question arises, "Why do so few of God's children enjoy a sweet communion with His Spirit?" Why is it that so many feel so "dry" in prayer? Dry lives come from dry prayer. Why is it that many have a difficult time feasting on the Scriptures? Malnutrition comes from not sucking the nutrients out of the Scriptures. Why is it so rare to find a Christian that has been so overtaken by communion with the Spirit, that all of his other interests have shriveled away? I ask you, dear reader, in all honesty, can you say that the life that you live is animated by a delightful, daily, divine exchange with God? Is the person of Christ really a present experience in your reading of the Scriptures? I wish to explore communion with God as the source of life.

A friend of mine once asked me, "How do you discipline yourself to spend days locked away from civilization with just a jug of water and a Bible? I pray for forty-five minutes and I am fresh out of things to say." I submit to you, as I did to my dear friend, that the first mistake in this question is the assumption that prayer is words. Prayer is not words. To think that prayer is words is like thinking love is a hug. It can be expressed through a hug, but it is a far deeper reality. Words are an expression of prayer, but prayer is far deeper. If prayer was words, then Paul was encouraging the life of a jabber when he wrote, "Pray without ceasing."

Prayer can be an endless, uninterrupted exchange and interaction and transaction with God. Prayer is simply the soul's total fixation upon God. I love what Michael Koulianos points out in Matthew

> **Prayer is simply the soul's total fixation upon God.**

chapter 6: Jesus in His discourse on prayer said, "When you pray, say...." He established the state of prayer before the speaking. Friends, it is imperative to recognize what prayer is if we are to ever experience God in it. Henry Scougal, the writer of the incredible classic, *The Life of God in the Soul of Man*, said, "Prayer is a state of the heart." Very simple, it is a posturing of your inner attention upon God. Madame Guyon said, "Prayer is the application of the heart to God." This is also a simplification, applying your affections to Him. Evagrius Ponticus said, "Prayer is the intercourse of Spirit with God." This is perfect to emphasize the exchange of communion with God. Intercourse of Spirit with God is a blend of man and God. Man's worthlessness mixed with God's infinite worth.

My friend's second mistake is that prayer is a matter of sheer discipline. Though there is a measure of discipline, the constant rejection of the old man that will always be present, prayer is hardly a stress upon the soul. Though I know that there exists deep intercession through a united heart with God's pain for a suffering humanity, prayer that I am addressing is communion with God; the exchange with God. Leonard Ravenhill said, "Prayer is agonizing soul sweat." I agree, intercession is a deeply burdened exercise of a heart united with God's.

My belief is that intercession and the sharing of God's heart issue out of sweet ecstasy with Him. The ecstasy produces the agony. A man and a woman experience each other in ecstasy and then the product is agony of childbirth. Intercession is a must, but it issues out of a disposition of joy and peace rooted in the inward gaze of the soul upon God. Prayer, true prayer, is the greatest delight of all. Prayer is inhaling the atmosphere of God's person. Dr. Michael L. Brown used to say that "prayer has a wonderfully addictive power to it. The more you pray, the more you want to pray." So my dear friend's mistake was, above all, a misconception of what prayer is.

So one may ask, "That is wonderful that prayer is that way for you, but what about me?" Or how about this one, "That is just not for everybody"? You might be saying, "I want that, but reading the Bible is like chewing on an old rope, and praying is boring as middle school homework." Brothers and sisters, it is our highest purpose to commune with God. If one thing is perfected in this life, let it be this. If our energies are channeled in any direction, let it be directly at Him. If we accomplish one thing, let it be a life lived in His presence in unbroken communion.

> **If we accomplish one thing, let it be a life lived in His presence in unbroken communion.**

Prayer is a not difficult ladder of performance or a hoop to jump through. Prayer is not searching for the proper calculation to unlock the gate of heaven. We must recognize that to experience God in prayer, after seeing what prayer is, is God's desire for us. Prayer is understood to be the sustained fixation of the soul upon God. We must recognize that the blood that poured out from the flesh of the God-man was to rent the veil over our eyes, so that we could have an endless vision of Jesus. That is what prayer is, "looking unto Jesus."[51] This is the reconciliation; God and man in direct fellowship. The reconciliation is the restoration of God and man finding pleasure in each other. Did you read that word, "pleasure"?

> **I submit to you that not only can prayer be a great delight, but it should be the very source of all our delight.**

So many people have no idea that communion with God can be a great delight. I submit to you that not only can prayer be a great delight, but it should be the very source of all our delight. John Ruusbroec wrote, "When God pleases us and we please God, therein is the practice of love and eternal life." God's desire is to be your greatest desire.

---

[51] Hebrews 12:1-2

His greatest delight is to be all your delight. John Piper once rephrased part of the Westminster confession as, "The chief end of man is to glorify God by finding pleasure in Him."

If these secrets are hidden from our eyes, it is only hidden because they are too simple for us. Madame Guyon wrote, "Prayer is as easy as breathing." Experiencing God in prayer is not a lottery. Nor should it be an exception to the rule. For many Christians, their most sensible experience of God was stumbled upon in the midst of an extreme situation that caused them to press through into a place of peace and rest they never had before. Or maybe they point back to an incredible moment where God used a man (as God loves to do) to bring the dew of heaven into their life.

But experiencing God is not just our refuge in the time of trouble, or the peace that we found while pressing in for breakthrough in a rough time. Rather, and this may be extreme to some or even foolish to others, experiencing God should be our daily source of life. Meaning, without a daily experience of God we do not live. "Man shall not live by bread alone, but by every word that proceeds out of the mouth of God" shows us the current living, speaking of God. Notice the text is not written as "which proceeded," but that which "proceeds."

His spoken words are still living and still speaking because they are Christ and Spirit. The early Christian theologians and mystics believed in an endless begetting of the Son of God as the Word. The Living Word said Himself, "I am the bread that comes down from heaven."

He is Himself an endless vision and in the same moment an endless speaking.

Notice He did not say, "came down." He is a perpetual speaking, unlike human words. God's speaking is an individual that is also Him. "God in these last days has spoken through His Son."[52] Everything that He is going to say and has said is now wrapped up in a person who is alive, and not only houses

---

[52] Hebrews 1:1

God's words, but is God's speaking. He is Himself an endless vision and in the same moment an endless speaking.

What do I mean? I mean, without Him, experienced in that wonderful way that makes it the best each time, the man feels lifeless and dead. I submit to you, that without an experience of God every day, we reduce our relationship with God to a practice of religion or devotional disciplines as lifeless as the Latter-day Saint down the road. I feel very strongly about this topic, and I have been extremely opposed for it. In following the Lord these last seventeen years I have, as many of you have as well, seen men of God slide back into their foolishness of sin and doubt.

I have seen anointed men of God reduce themselves to mere orators. I have seen joy-filled brothers and sisters now bogged down with depression and death all over them. Do you want to know what each of these has in common, though all from different walks of life, many of them ministers or completely changed in the heat of an incredible move of the Spirit through the Gospel? In every case, without fail, there was a slipping away from the communion with God. God became replaced by theological arguments or studies for the sake of knowledge. God was replaced with a girlfriend or a boyfriend. God began to be eclipsed by work, family, ministry, friends, hobbies, and many other things. He was no longer a delight, but a duty. He became a religious devotion instead of a river of delight. Being with Him was no longer the bliss of life but the loss of the fulfillment of self-desires.

> **I am saying that communion with God is the greatest ineffable joy of life and the source of every bliss.**

What am I saying? I am saying that communion with God is the greatest ineffable joy of life and the source of every bliss. If it is not this way for you, no matter how much you minister, or preach on the street, or seek miracles, or love the gathering of the saints in conferences and prayer meetings, you are running on empty and it is only a matter of time before you wake up and say to yourself, "What am I doing? I am miserable. I seriously just want to gratify myself and ask for forgiveness later. I believe in Him enough to not turn my back completely, but to say that Christ experienced in my life is the core reason of my existence, would be a lie."

Brother, let me tell you, you cannot fool God. He knows if your desire really is with the lusts of this age or if He truly is your pleasure and pursuit. Though I know that many reading this are not living in a exhilarating experience of Jesus daily, I know God is raising up the Jesus people who live in a whole other place of unceasing delight in God, that distinguishes them from the rest. Here is, what I believe, the main "simple secret" to a daily and continuous experience of God, because of Jesus Christ through the Holy Spirit to be.

> **I know God is raising up the Jesus people who live in a whole other place of unceasing delight in God, that distinguishes them from the rest.**

ɔme to Him. Jesus said, "Come unto Me—come and continually come to Me." He tells us to "Drink and keep on drinking." It is a continuous experience of Him. Come to Him—not your Bible, not communion, not your iPod, not your journal, not a book or devotional, not to your prayer list, not to an audio sermon or a YouTube message by your favorite preacher, not a time of daily planning or a solitary thorough thinking session with God—come to Him and only Him.

Coming to Him, does it not imply coming only for Him? What I mean by that is, coming to connect and remain connected with Him as the sole object of prayer and life, must be the reality of our life. How do I "come to Him"? It means, give Him your heart—all your attention, all of your gaze, all of your surrendered will—resting in the fact that He wants to be with you and He has washed your sins away by the death of His own Son. It means, turn all over to Him in trust and yielded affection, tossing out all the expectations of what you want Him to do for you, or what you want to do for Him. Burn all those systematic prayer routines out of your mind. Just come to Him, and just simply be there.

How? Let your soul approach Him, with or without words and no matter what state your heart is in, lay your existence at His feet in loving thanksgiving and you will find your soul drift into adoration. Let me say this again: Just come to Him to be with Him. Come to Him

> **Waiting is simply remaining still in adoration until the wind and will of the Spirit blow you into a specific direction.**

with the goal of simply adoring Him and remaining in the seeming nothingness of lost blissful, wordless worship.

In worship, words are like oxygen. The higher you ascend, the more absent they are. Come to Him, not to settle issues or get clarity on something—forget about all things concerning you. Let go of all those problems, questions, thoughts, worries, and self-centered fears. Just look at Him by the simple fixation of all your atten-tion upon Him and allow your heart to go up to Him in worshipful surrender and adoration.

Recognize this as the goal. Waiting is simply remaining still in adoration until the wind and will of the Spirit blow you into a specific direction. Here is the tender bliss of His presence that opens the Scriptures like an unfolding flower before the life rays of God. Here is where the Word of God will come alive. You are not waiting for anything else. The trees are still and their only movement is when the wind blows by. Let us learn from them how to worship God and live a life of obedience to God through the leading of the Spirit.

In all practicality, it is important to block out some time daily to simply be with Him. It would be good to at least have an hour or two of unbroken, uninterrupted concentration on Him. There is no real need for a lot of words. All He is really wanting is your heart's full attention. As a matter of fact, read this next line closely; it is the only way to actually sense Him. *If you have a very difficult time sensing the sweet presence of the Spirit alone with Him, I promise you that it is because of your lack of attention, scattered thinking, and inability to sustain your heart's gaze upon Him in stillness.* People easily rebuttal this thought by saying, "That is the efforts of man and you can't do anything to set God before you." Brother, we all have a soul that is scattered and self-centered, and to deny this fact is total self-deception.

So the scalpel to soulical submission to God that I have just described is universally true for all. Adoration is always the way in. Stillness is always the way to adoration. Surrender is always the way to stillness. Let me add that if I don't come to Him daily, the scatteredness of my soul will increase and it will become more difficult to get still. And if the soul does not get still, the flow of God will never sensibly pass through the Spirit into the experience of the soul.

> **Adoration is always the way in. Stillness is always the way to adoration. Surrender is always the way to stillness.**

It is that simple. Your experience will increase more and more as you practice a life of stillness and adoration alone with Him and throughout the day. For so long we have thought the phrase "in Him" as theological and positional. It is far more. It is an actual disposition of the soul that is sensitive to the sweet presence and moving of the Spirit. To abide in Him is to live in communion with Him.

Think of an ice cube in the sun. What slowly begins to take place is a change in form; it soon melts little by little under the rays of the sun. The liquid form of the water begins to flow and the direction that the water flows is based upon the ground that the ice rests on. This is much like the union of communion with the Spirit. Adoration is united with waiting in His presence even as the ice sits in stillness under the rays of the sun. The change of still form soon changes into the fluid of prayer that moves in direct accordance with the ground of the Word of God upon which everything rests. Communion with the Spirit is much like this. The divine knitting—Adoration is the clinging of the thread to the needle as the divine hand penetrates the Scriptures and pulls through them by prayer. So His Spirit knits us to Himself.

Adoration of Christ causes a manifestation of His presence, and in the manifestation of His presence we are granted the internal gracious disposition for realization of His word. Here enters meditation upon that word, resulting in a revelation of the person of Christ. Revelation is much more than understanding; it is an actual divine installation of His grace. This installation produces trans-

Revelation is much more than understanding; it is an actual divine installation of His grace.

formation in our lives. Part of the transformation is subordination to the loving, powerful reign of Christ in our hearts. With the Kingdom set up on the inside we are granted demonstration of His power through our proclamation of Christ. Adoration, manifestation, realization, meditation, revelation, installation, transformation, demonstration in proclamation.

As we adore Him and the presence begins to slightly manifest in sensible tranquility, ease, and peace, we turn our attention to His presence in adoration. That presence will begin to increase and end up swallowing our self-consciousness, making us free to be led by the Spirit without the distractions, delusions, deceptions, and diluting of self. Self is the biggest enemy of an ecstatic experience of God.

CHAPTER SEVEN

UNION IN COMMUNION II

"Every one who thirsts, come to the waters;
and you who have no money come, buy and eat.
Come, buy wine and milk without money and without
cost. Why do you spend money for what is not bread,
and your wages for what does not satisfy?
Listen carefully to Me, and eat what is good,
and delight yourself in abundance.
"Incline your ear and come to Me.
Listen, that you may live."
—Isaiah 55:1-3, NASB

I can hear the angelic oration of invitation from Lady Wisdom in the public square.[53] I can feel the bleeding heart of Christ universally crying out for all

---

[53] Proverbs 8

thirsty souls to come to Him and drink.[54] Isaiah is moved by the same Spirit to trumpet an identical summoning, *"Every one who thirsts, come to the waters...."* The invitation is universal, "Everyone...." Yet in the same instance, it is restricted. The invitation is for every thirsty soul. There is absolutely no prequalifying; all that is needed is thirst. For the conflagrating spokesman of God proclaims, *"Everyone who thirsts,* come to the waters...."

COME TO HIM

Do you know what it means to thirst? It is a self-evident truth that thirst is the body's recognition of its need for water. Thirst is personal, for you cannot thirst for another and no other can thirst for you. If you are simple and honest enough to recognize that your soul is in need, then there is only one thing to do, give in to His invitation. Herein lies the ease of prayer, the recognition that prayer is easy. Simply, yield to Him. There are no hoops to jump through or exceptional methods to follow, for God has made Himself as available as light shining through a window. He will come in to the degree that

---

[54] John 7

you will not obstruct Him.[55]
That is His personality. He
is totally in love with you,
longing always to be in
your gaze and to supply
your soul with strength,
joy, and love in His presence. Put behind you the

**He is totally in love
with you, longing
always to be
in your gaze
and to supply your
soul with strength,
joy, and love in
His presence.**

wind sprints of works and the competitive suspicions of
other people and recognize that there is only one way
into the quenching Fountain of Living Water, and that is
to "Come to Him."

It isn't any more complicated than this, to simply come
to the Waters. This is fellowship divine; to leave behind
all things, your failures, your victories, your disobedience, your self-consciousness, your wicked appetites,
and enter into His presence where His sweet voice illuminates the soul. Jesus says, "If anyone thirsts, let him
come to Me and drink." Oh, what joy to know that the
thirst-quenching water is Jesus Himself! Anyone who

---

[55] I heard this from Father Thomas Dubay, S. M., many years ago.

will recognize his constant need of Jesus can continually come and receive Him.

REMOVING THE HINDRANCES

Reader, the condition of your soul is irrelevant. You must understand this: Even if your heart is defiled and your sins rush over your head, come to Him. One cannot buy his way to God with good deeds or a clean living. Just as no amount of money or material possessions could ever purchase this water. Even our most moral, self-less, and benevolent act is shy of perfection's price. As Charles Spurgeon wrote, "The lips of the harlot are just as accepted as the lips of the king upon the chalice of God."[56] That is the nature of His grace. Grace is always without merit. This is how we came to Him and this is how we continually come to Him.

My friend, this is how one buys without money. This is the acceptable currency of exchange: the thirst of the soul. It is the recognition of one's own poverty that breaks

---

[56] C. H. Spurgeon, *Morning and Evening* (Scotland, UK: Christian Focus Publications, 1994), 762.

the ego down and casts away pride, so that man may simply come to Him. Again, I say, poverty is the only currency. Pride is man's longing to perform something himself. Pride is man's striving in religious attempts to please God with the efforts of the Adamic life. Pride is Adam without Christ and spiritual pride is Adam trying in his own strength to look like Christ. There is no plan for the old man, but

> **Pride is Adam without Christ and spiritual pride is Adam trying in his own strength to look like Christ.**

execution. Pride is Adam's refusal to collapse under Christ's perfect blood sacrifice sewing together fig leaves to cover himself.[57] Pride is presenting to God the fruit of the earth, which man was made from, instead of the only substance acceptable to God, the blood of the Innocent Other.[58]

Oh, the one who lays down his pride and recognizes that he does not have in himself now, or ever, what he most

---

[57] Genesis 3
[58] Genesis 4

severely needs! Oh, how magnetic is the life that drags its sinful, broken, arrogant, and filthy soul to the feet of Jesus! With such a currency, any man can buy without price, the Bread of Life. With this currency alone God is well pleased, because through such a currency God's currency is activated. It is through the recognition of one's own poverty and need, casting himself down at Christ's pierced feet, that he can purchase drink for his thirsty soul. Such is the water to quench and the bread to satisfy. And as Paul asked the Galatians, "How did you receive the Spirit?"[59] Was it not by faith? Faith is the refusal to trust ourselves, casting our all upon God in absolute trust. Poverty is the ground of faith and faith is the action of poverty. Poverty's price is the only way to purchase the wine of the intoxicating influence of God's Spirit that separates man from self-consciousness and drowns him in God consciousness. Poverty also, supplies

> **It is through the recognition of one's own poverty and need, casting himself down at Christ's pierced feet, that he can purchase drink for his thirsty soul.**

---

[59] Galatians 3:2

for the soul the "milk of the Word" filled with all the nutrients for spiritual growth.[60]

With such a universal offer of drink, food, wine, and milk,
to him who recognizes he has no money, no value in and
of himself, the question arises, "Why spend money for
those things that are not bread and do not satisfy?" Sin
will never satisfy and neither will religion. Why waste
yourself in prideful independence and religious efforts
pressing, turning, manipulating, and striving for things
that will never be satisfaction to your soul? In contrast
to this multiplicity of life and frustrated striving, give
yourself to the passivity of listening in humble, wholehearted attentiveness to God's voice. Take time to listen
carefully.[61]

To listen to someone is to remove your attention from all
other things and concentrate all attention upon the individual that is speaking to you. As Evagrius of Pontus

---

[60] 1 Peter 2:2; 2 Peter 3:18

[61] The references in the Scripture concerning the importance of
listening are too numerous to site.

wrote, "Nothing is more essential to prayer than concentration."[62] Then you will receive sustaining bread, divine food, which is good for the soul. Christ as bread is complete spiritual nutrition.[63] This is the delight of the soul in abundance. For Christ is the never-ending food storage for God to feed us from the endless supply of Himself. We are born of the Word. Our new life is the internal residence of the Word and we nourish that life by the continual reception of that same living substance of the Word of Life.

> **We are born of the Word. Our new life is the internal residence of the Word and we nourish that life by the continual reception of that same living substance of the Word of Life.**

"The unsearchably rich Christ is a feast prepared by God for man's enjoyment."[64] God became man that He might dispense Himself into man through the divine mingling

---

[62] J. A. McGuckin, *The Book of Mystical Chapters* (Massachusetts: Shambhala Publications, 2002), 37.

[63] John 6:51

[64] Witness Lee, *The Tree of Life* (Anaheim, CA: Living Stream Ministries, 1987), 104.

of humanity and divinity as the soul feasts upon the Lord Himself.

ATTENTION

Everyone who thirsts, "incline your ear," simply give all of your attention to God. Still your scattered soul and look unto Jesus, gazing intently with adoration on the beauty of God. This, my friend, is coming unto Jesus without price, humbly living at His feet and receiving Him as the all satisfying water, bread, wine, and milk.

We receive Christ as all, not just for salvation from the lusts and systems of this world, and not only from the deception of the self-life, but we receive Him to live life in the joy and bliss of Salvation Himself.[65] For Christ is all; water for the thirsty soul, bread for the hungry heart, wine of pleasure, and the nutritious milk of the Word. God imperatively inscribes through Isaiah the summary of all of life, "Listen that you may live." Life is found in the soul's passively gazing in still adoration, with full attention upon God, waiting upon His voice. For the Word

---

[65] Psalm 27:1

from the mouth of God, by the breath of the Spirit of God, is God Himself imparted into man, both satisfying and unifying the soul with God.

QUOTES AND NOTES

"The wind of heaven only carries the yielded soul."

"Children trust their Father, but sons are trusted
by their Father."

"Don't seek to become something,
but rather to be only His."

"Praise is verbal trust in the face of
your earthly circumstance."

"Do you want to know when your fire goes out?
When you stop giving it something to burn."

"Holiness is the fruit of being addicted to the maximum
pleasure of life, which is God Himself."

"Nobody gets pregnant holding hands. Getting intimate
with Jesus is the only way to be fruitful."

"God's voice comes out of His face."

"If we seek Him for power we forfeit intimacy."

"Jesus was unyielding to the rich ruler because there is simply no way to obtain divine life through morality; only subjectivity to Jesus."

"Remember the one condition: habitual, unceasing, absolute dependence upon Him."
—*Andrew Murray*

"For Paul, the Spirit, as an experienced and living reality, was the absolute crucial matter for the Christian life, from beginning to end."
—*Gordon Fee*

"If I love God alone, I will desire God alone."
—*Madame Guyon*

"For Paul, joy is one of the most certain hallmarks of genuine spirituality."
—*Gordon Fee*

"When the rule of God is in the soul, then the kingdom is within."

"You have to have taken your eyes off Jesus to look at another."

"The statement of our lives should clearly be: He came, He is here, and He's coming."

"God is so in love with His people, and His voice is in everything that He does."
—*Brian Guerin*

"The reconciliation is the restoration of God and man finding pleasure in each other."

"Internal unrest is the warning of the Holy Ghost."

"Healthy tension between divine activity and human responsibility runs throughout Paul's letters."
—*Gordon Fee*

"Do not fall into the trap of thinking that Christ-likeness doesn't necessitate miracles."

"Stay with me, Jesus, if you wish me to be faithful to You."
—*St. Padre Pio*

"The Christian battle is nothing more than fighting to sustain that simple, helpless trust we had the first day He saved us."

"Salvation, for Paul, was primarily an eschatological reality, begun with Christ's coming, to be consummated by His soon return."
—*Gordon Fee*

"Neglect is one of the greatest assassins
of the spiritual life."

"He would read a book until he heard God
speak to him. Then he would put the book down
and just listen to God."
—*Spoken of A. W. Tozer*

"He has kissed you with the kisses of His mouth, and
killed your doubts by the closeness of His embrace."
—*C. H. Spurgeon*

"No freshly spoken word of God will ever
come to you that doesn't already contain its
own ability to perform itself."
—*Bill Johnson*

"The first step away from God is...
lack of desire for those things for which the soul
hungers when it longs for God."
—*Monk Motto*

"Every time you are in personal contact with Jesus,
His words are real to you."
—*Oswald Chambers*

"Inactivity is seen as the greatest activity in the plan of
God: spending time alone with the Lord."
—*K. P. Yohannan*

"The unceasing reception of God produces an ecstatic preoccupation with Jesus alone."

"If we ignore the impressions of the Spirit, soon we will no longer be able to sense them."

"The Christian life that isn't satisfied with God alone, testifies to the world that God is not enough."

"The Old Testament was a high and lofty standard and the New Testament is a high and lofty Christ."
—*David Popovici*

"Concerning healing—it is not about attainment but atonement."

"Isn't it funny that in His hometown they couldn't know Jesus because they knew Jesus."
—*Bill Johnson*

"He asks not so much for our service as our communion."
—*A. B. Simpson*

"'Abide in Me and I in You.' When the man makes a decision to dwell in God, then God can make His residence in that man."

"Jesus cannot teach us anything until we quiet all our intellectual questions and get alone with Him."
—*Oswald Chambers*

"The reason that a constant experience of God is so rare
is because scattered minds are so common."

"Do you want to know if you are really a servant
of God? It is how you respond when you are
treated like a servant."
—*Unknown*

"Beware of the barrenness of a busy life."
—*Corrie ten Boom*

"Never crank it. But if the Lord starts the engine,
ride it as long as you can."
—*John Kilpatrick*

"I pray for a jealousy to grip us, to ruthlessly reject
anything that would seek to draw our attention away
from unbroken communion with God."

"In order to Love Him with ALL my heart,
it means I must let go of ALL OTHER loves."
—*Mother Basilea Schlink*

"Regard one another as more important
than yourselves."
—*St. Paul*

"Some people are looking for God to revise the Church,
but we need Him to revive the Church."

"To lack joy is to be drawing from a foreign source."

"O, sweetness and beauty everlasting, you have
wounded my heart.... I am scarcely alive,
for I die in the face of joy...."
—*Richard Rolle*

"People ask me how to see miracles and I say bring
your heart to a place where you can say,
'Lord have mercy on me.'"
—*Nathan Morris*

"You cannot receive anything from Jesus until Jesus
becomes real to you."
—*Benny Hinn*

"When you are not spiritually hungry, that is the day
you are spiritually dead."
—*Benny Hinn*

"The Living Presence is life and cannot be separated
from continual experience."

"One of the greatest spiritual principles I have ever
heard is by Bill Johnson, 'Whatever you
give attention to, grows.'"

"Am I sleeping while my Savior is dying?
Lord, teach me how to pray."
—*Jason Upton*

"If your doctrine doesn't lead to a daily experience
of God, it's false doctrine."
—*Michael Koulianos*

"I've yet to see a doctrine heal the sick."
—*Michael Koulianos*

"My friend Daniel asked Arthur Burk what his favorite
thing about Jesus is, to which he replied, 'That He is the
expression of another.'"

"Think on this...the All-Seeing One consented
to be blindfolded."

"In ministry, our comfort must rest in the Person
that we have been with—not in the amount
of our preparation."

"Out of revival alone springs a vanguard of men who
will eagerly hazard their lives for His dear sake."
—*Leonard Ravenhill*

"One of the most powerful things the Holy Spirit ever
taught me in prayer was, 'Ssshhhhh.'"

"What you do in private, God will reveal publicly."
—*John Kilpatrick*

"Hence, the soul has to authorize the spirit to rule before the Spirit can rule over the soul and the body." (The soul has to yield to the spirit man, who is one with the Holy Spirit. The Holy Spirit rules the soul of man through the Spirit of man.)
—*Watchman Nee* (parentheses added)

"To love Him constantly, my heart must see Him constantly."
—*Michael Koulianos*

"A man's greatest and highest goal in life is to enjoy intimate communion with Christ."
—*Phillip Keller*

"A calm hour with God is worth a lifetime with any man."
—*Robert Murray McCheyne*

"People often ask me, 'Michael, what do you when you pray?' My response is, 'Hopefully, I do nothing.'"
—*Michael Koulianos*

"Too many of us have a Christian vocabulary rather than a Christian experience."
—*Charles F. Banning*

"A casket or a Bible. Pick one."
—*God's word to Kenneth Hagin when He called him into the ministry*

"God's identification with man and man's identification with God are by the same means—the cross."
—*David Popovici*

"You can love the truth of a person and still not have the experience of that person. But only by experience can that person be known."

"It isn't hard to see Jesus. You just have to learn to relax in the Spirit."
—*Ruth Ward Heflin*

"We cannot carry the river. The river carries us."
—*Ruth Ward Heflin*

"Idolatry is what we do when we decide that we do not want to wait anymore."

"Worship destroys worry."

"The King is the Kingdom. I'd rather live a thousand hells with Him than heaven without Him."
—*David Popovici*

"The tension of hunger and satisfaction in God is that each time God fills the cup, He simultaneously expands its holding capacity."

"If we are not careful, our desire for an inspirational legacy or reputation can be our fuel, in the place of a heart captivated by Jesus."

"Stillness—the magnetic force to the
frequencies of God."
—*Brian Guerin*

"Moses did not know the skin of his face shone because
of His speaking with him (God). We shine when we
receive God's voice."

"Both the humility to not see the glory on himself and
the glory itself came from the same place—
communion with the Lord."

"Jesus is sweets and meat at the same time.
His honey is the way to wisdom."
—*See Proverbs 24:13, 14*

"The presence is in the present."

"God uses men who are weak and feeble
enough to lean on Him."
—*Hudson Taylor*

"He became powerless to make me powerful."
—*Richard Rolle*

"Communion with the Holy Spirit
will always yield a preached Jesus."
—*Michael Koulianos*

"A spiritual Christian is one who allows the Holy Spirit to operate within his spirit."
—*Watchman Nee*

"Everything Paul touches turns to gospel."
—*Gordon Fee*

"As Thou hast been, Thou forever will be."
—*from the hymn, "Great Is Thy Faithfulness"*

"Sobriety in the Kingdom looks like intoxication with His presence."
—*David Popovici*

"Those inebriated by the blood of Calvary are the most sober in this life."
—*David Popovici*

"He doubly showed His humility, both by what He put off and what He put on."
—*Robert Govet*

"He 'emptied' Himself as the Son of God; He 'humbled' Himself as the son of man."
—*Robert Govet*

"There is no pleasure of His presence without surrender, just as sure as there is no resurrection without death."

"It seems to always be the men without power in Christianity that come against those men with power."

"Anyone who has experienced Jesus knows that He is sweet as honey, never growing old, always healing the soul, and comforting in everything."

"The trees of the field clap their hands when the Wind has blown on them. This is true praise."

"Paul has none of our hang-ups over whether a Spirit person can receive the Spirit."
—*Gordon Fee*

"They who make idols are like them (without the Spirit of life); so are all those who trust in them."
—*Psalm 115:8*

"We adopt the nature of whatever we place our trust in."

"A life of experiential union is dependent upon continual loss of self."

"Those who love Jesus seek His presence with an agony of desire."
—*Charles Spurgeon*

"I can't imagine after all His faithfulness and love throughout our lives, that any of us will have an appetite at the marriage supper of the Lamb."

"Christ was supplying air for the soldiers to breath as they nailed Him to the cross."

"The fruit you bear will correspond to the time spent in true prayer."
—*Mother Basilea Schlink*

"Loving Jesus is enough."
—*Michael Koulianos*

"If we don't put each other above ourselves and prefer each other, our wisdom can't demonstrate the power of the cross."

"It is because Jesus has taken hold of me, and because Jesus keeps me, that I dare to say:
'Savior, I abide in You.'"
—*Andrew Murray*

"Every day, Jesus is the same, the wonderful flowing fountain of life and pleasure; the only source of joy and peace and love."

"Only by pleasure in Christ can we endure pain for Christ."

"If my heart slips into busyness, I immediately and unbearably miss Jesus."

"Devotion apart from infusion is religion."

"Worry makes no sense."

"Our God is a shoreless sea of pleasure."
—*A. W. Tozer*

"Men are bent against pleasure in the Spirit to the degree that they don't experience it."

"The reason the devil presses the people of God away from rest and pleasure in God is because he knows those elements create a Holy Bride."

"When you fear the Lord you will make wise decisions."
—*Dr. Jeff Hubing*

"I want no advice from a rocking chair."
—*Reinhard Bonnke*

"I will open the Sudan to the Gospel or die trying."
—*Rowland Bingham*

"If Song of Solomon is telling us anything, it is that commitment, adoration, and ecstatic experience is the affectionate love relationship with Jesus."

"Marriage is the greatest tool in life to conquer those things that need to be conquered in you."
—*Danielle Popovici*

"Whatever it costs to have a godly home, we'll pay it."
—*Danielle Popovici*

"If I win the whole world and I lose my kids,
I feel like I lose in the end."
—*Danielle Popovici*

"Anybody that can't take correction still needs to be
delivered from rejection."
—*Tony Kemp*

"Nothing is more satanic than to seek to be like the
Most High apart from the Spirit."

"You corrupted your wisdom by reason...."
—*Ezekiel 28:17*

"We experience His presence because of the cross. If He
removed the experience of His presence from us, then
He reverses the cross's work."

"If I could bestow any gift on you tonight, I would
bestow the gift of spiritual hunger."
—*John G. Lake*

"Fix your heart on Christ and He will seize it to Himself
and protect it from the infection of worldly enterprises."
—*Richard Rolle*

"Only Christ Himself can call us to follow Him."
—*Bonheoffer*

"God's greatest pleasure is when He
is our only pleasure."

"Discipline will break us into some things, but
surrender alone will enter the glory."

"We feel the need to prove ourselves when
our opinion of ourselves is of a higher quality
than what we in fact are."

"I will not be a citizen where Jesus was an alien."
—*Charles Spurgeon*

"The 'Law of the Spirit' means that now transgression is
not obeying the Spirit's voice."

"You will catch a lot more flies with one spoon of honey
than a barrel of vinegar."
—*Charles Spurgeon*

"The gavel is a good incentive, but only the wine of the
Spirit will make us wholly His."

"The world out there is not dying because of the
strength of humanism, but the weakness of evangelism."
—*Leonard Ravenhill*

"In the Spirit life, thirst and drink are continually
contingent upon each other."

"Without His presence in our lives, our hearts
are home here; but in His presence, we are strangers.
'I am a stranger WITH THEE.'"
—*King David*

"The upright live in His presence."
—*Psalm 140*

"To the yielded heart God gives the sensible experience
of His love in His presence. 'Let Him kiss me...
love is better than wine.'"
—*Song 1:2*

"Fasting is the soul's focused feast on
the all-satisfying Christ."
—*John Piper*

"The believer can each day be pleasing to God
only in that which he does through the power
of Christ dwelling in him."
—*Andrew Murray*

"God will not share the throne of your heart
with a principle."

"The devil hates and oppresses the experience
of Christ in Christianity because it transforms
our information into a relationship."

"The seduction is to set our affection and attention on
something, anything, besides the groom, Jesus."
—*See 2 Corinthians 11:3*

"I am convinced that God keeps giants in the land to
keep us dependent upon Him."

"Pride is seeking the externals of God without the internals of God."

"The aroma of Christ's person is only experienced when the breeze of the Spirit blows on Him toward you."

"Three main reason why not to sin: 1. It grieves the Holy Spirit; 2. It saps my desire for God; 3. It callouses my sense of His presence."

"If our 'positional standing' in Christ takes away the potential for darkness, then we will theologically abandon consistent dependency."

"The thing that makes religious people most angry is when God possesses a man."

"If we cease our activity in His presence, we will slip into His."

"If you want the flow of the grace of God to wane in your life, simply judge someone."

"What is 'walking in the light'? It is unbroken fellowship with the Father."

"Spiritual nature, like bodily nature, will be served; deny it food and it will gobble poison."
—*C.S. Lewis*

"The moment I turn to Him, it is like turning on an electric current which I feel through my whole being."
—*Brother Lawrence*

"Worship Him until you are aware of His presence. Then give all your attention to the intoxication of His presence and you will find rest from fear, striving, worry, and pain."

"Part of the reason most Christians are not eager to give people what they have is because what they have doesn't really satisfy them."

"Come away out of self and its life, abide in Christ and the Christ life, and Christ will be your life."
—*Andrew Murray*

"They didn't need to tie Jesus to the whipping post. He would have held on for every one of us."
—*Michael Koulianos*

"Sometimes the pain that we feel in the midst of trial is due to our investment in this world."

"Affliction has a way of spoiling that which would have otherwise spoiled us."
—*Unknown*

"Faith is our walk, but fellowship sensibly felt is our rest."
—*Charles Spurgeon*

"To be unspiritual means that things other than Christ have a growing fascination for you."
—*Oswald Chambers*

"When you become hasty and anxious, it is an alarm to your soul that you are in need of His voice."

"Why is wisdom pictured as a woman? Because, only women can bear children; her children vindicate her. Real wisdom has real fruit."

"The Christian hedonists seek pleasure; the Christian mystics seek oneness. Not the same."

"Enjoying prayer is blocked by our need to accomplish something. The sweetest prayer is enjoyed by simply being there in sustained surrender."

"Practice until the eye of your heart will be constantly inclined upward."
—*Richard Rolle*

"Joy in suffering means our happiness doesn't come from what is happening to us."

"Signs and wonders are an undeniable divine attestation to the deity of Christ (Acts 2:22). No wonder they are so opposed."

"If you come to Him for something other than Him, you will miss Him."

"We can tell how much we love His presence
by how uncomfortable we are when we are unaware
of His presence."

"Craving God means an unceasing longing and
simultaneous dwelling in His presence."

"Break the spell of any Gnostic charmer....
He who sins is of the devil."
—*A. T. Robertson*

"The heart of Christianity is mysticism; Spirit contact
with God in Christ by the Holy Spirit."
—*A. T. Robertson*

"...the truth is IN Jesus."
—*Ephesians 4*

"There isn't a scalpel thin enough to divide Christ
and His presence."

"O, Wisest Madness, may I never live without You."
—*St. Alphonsus*

"Someone asked me, 'Why do you listen to that kind of
worship music over and over?' I answered, 'I love the
GLORY more than my personal taste in music.'"

"To get closer to my wife, I don't stop talking to her,
leave her for a while—then return to see if she
still loves me. Dryness is not God."

"...the rebellious dwell in dryness."
—*Psalm 68.6*

"Arrogance is heightened when we claim faithfulness apart from dependence upon His presence."

"He is a never-drying fountain."
—*Donna Alley*

"A method has no power nor effect; for not being Christ, it is simply a dead thing. Every spiritual thing outside of Christ is dead."
—*Watchman Nee*

"Jesus, the great substitute, was in the stead of man, not just for His sickness and sin, but His distance from God's presence."

"Song of Songs forever settles the fact that God is a continuous experience. Her sin and sloth were her only two instances of distance."

Jonathan Edwards on the people during revival, "...their doubts were removed by a more satisfying experience."

"The doctrine of God-ordained dryness is a direct and disrespectful assault on Christ's words in John 4:14, "...will never thirst.""

151

"How easily we Christians forget our own sins and recall the sins of others. He who shows mercy will be shown mercy."

"I will not cover the flame in my heart to make cold hearts feel comfortable."

"Beware of any identity in Christ that doesn't strip down, pick up a towel, and wash the feet of others."

"Christianity is not a change of life but an exchange of life."

"There is no such thing as interaction with God that fails to make you like Him."

"Mysticism is the attempt to communicate the incommunicable; to bring to speech a consciousness of the direct presence of God."
—*Bernard McGinn*

"To deny that the River is flowing is to deny that the Rock has been struck. The River is flowing because the Rock has been struck!"

"If you hesitate to obey, it will sap the strength of the Word."

"Abandonment is the casting away of all selfish care that we may be all together at the divine disposal."
—*Madame Guyon*

"Any time the passions are turbulent,
a gentle retreat inwards unto a present God,
easily deadens and pacifies them."
—*Madame Guyon*

"The religious devils seek to take the place
of the Holy Ghost."
—*David Hogan*

"Deception is germinal."

"When you really tap into His sweetness through
stillness and adoration that leads into reception, there
is no difference between a scarecrow and a stripper."

"What we need most in order to make spiritual
progress is to be silent before God; the language
He best hears is silent love."
—*St. John of the Cross*

"God has no communion with unbelief."

"May all my mistakes in life only be a stepping-stone to
others that would bring them closer to Jesus."
—*William Branham*

"It is that inexplicable feeling of satisfaction in His
presence which enables us to finish our course."
—*Watchman Nee*

"There is nothing remotely close to the rapturous delight of being in silence and solitude for an extended period of time to simply be His."

"Empty stimuli kills the receptivity of the soul."
—*Thomas Dubay*

"HE WHO IS FROM ABOVE IS ABOVE ALL."
—*John the Baptist*

"Concerning an early influence in our lives, a brother said, 'You used to feel the anointing drip off his tongue; now all you find is knowledge.'"

"The period of the fast was spent in spiritual ecstasy, during which the wants of the natural body were suspended."
—*Alford on Matthew 4*

"The devil didn't come to Jesus with a pornographic magazine, but a subtle appeal to use His own will."

"Two demonic strategies: To take you out of the moment you are in—God's presence is in the present; To distract you with innocent things."

"Satan seeks to bombard you with the innocent to rob you of the valuable."

"If you have the smile of God, what does it matter if you have the frown of men?"
—*Leonard Ravenhill*

"Only if our works issue out of rest can we be sure that they originate in God."

"The presence is only in the present. Godliness is mastering the momentary enjoyment of God."

Concerning Christ, present in the depths of the Scriptures: "Bees can only draw the juice from the flowers by resting on them, not by flying around them."
—*Madame Guyon*

"In prayer, as you wait in His presence,
He will come underneath you like wind and take you where you need to go."

"The root of the marred image of Jesus in the Church is a lack of satisfaction in God."

"...I don't want to offend His Spirit by just rushing on."
—*Lindell Cooley*

"A dungeon with Christ is a throne, and a throne without Christ is a hell."
—*Martin Luther*

"At a wedding I heard the minister say a phrase that brought tears to my eyes '…forsaking all others.' God, give us bridal love!'"

"Only in rest upon His breast do we access the divine treasure chest."

"Once we have tasted God, it is impossible
to delight in anything but Him."
—*Madame Guyon*

"He is more eager to give Himself to us
than we are to possess Him."
—*Madame Guyon*

"Three words Jesus says every day: 'Come to Me.'"

"Give every spare second to God."
—*Fenelon*

"Prayer's power and effectiveness rest
on union with Jesus."
—*See John 15:7-8*

"Be strong in the Lord means: you are empowered
through union with Him."

"Faith is…the submission of the mind."
—*Mary of the Holy Trinity*

"I am so filled with joy and happiness that I am amazed
my soul stays in my body."
—*St. Catherine of Siena*

"Take this heart, burn and rive (tear, split or cleave)
this heart, my Jesus."
—*St. Joseph of Cupertino*

"Where are those who love Me simply because I am the
Savior, because I am your God and your All?"
—*Jesus to Mary of the Holy Trinity*

"The union of man with God consists not in a confusion
of natures (the divine with the human),
but in a conformity of wills."
—*St. Bernard of Clairvaux*

"There exists no greater teacher on the inner life than
extended seasons of solitude in stillness and silence,
waiting in His presence."

"Only if we love the idea of God more than
the Person of God will we set our hearts against
the experience of God."

"In the reception of His voice is the power to obey it."

"It is in the process of being worshipped that God
communicates His presence to men."
—*C. S. Lewis*

"It is in the sweet nothingness of fixed,
still waiting in His presence in adoration where
the great somethings happen."

"The first purpose of trials and tribulations is
to remind you that the sole source of your joy and peace
is sweet fellowship with Jesus."

"The word 'if' is the beautiful evidence of God
bestowing free will in the human soul."

"Proverbs shows us, listening to the voice of the Father
drowns out the voice of the seductress."

"God is more interested in making the man
than he is in making his ministry."
—*David Popovici*

"Whatever realm you are more aware of will determine
which one satisfies you most."
—*Colossians 3:1*

"With regard to chastity, I believe him to be angelic."
—*Father Lorenzo questioned by investigators
on the life of Padre Pio*

"God loves His praying men so much that
He allows them to bear His name, and even in their
flaws He puts His face in theirs."

"Sometimes an extended time of sustained, restful, still adoration in silence is the only thing that will break the activity of the soul."

Curé d'Ars says concerning prayer,
"I look at God and He looks at me."

"The more you pray, the more you love to pray."
—*Curé d'Ars*

"Prayer was the greatest joy of his soul
and his habitual refuge."
—*Commentator on the life of Curé d'Ars*

"In a soul united to God, it is always springtime."
—*Curé d'Ars*

"Ministry is people seeing God through
your living in God."

"Following Jesus means forsaking all other
nourishments and forever resigning to only eat
of the Bread of Life."

Curé d'Ars was, "...forever pursued by
a desire for solitude."
—*Francis Trochu*

"Any study of revival will show us that evangelism
is not revival but rather a result of it."

"One indispensible commonality between all my personal favorite wonder-working heroic friends of God: they spent insane amounts of time with Him."

"God doesn't heal the heart by theology but by wine."

"Many Christians that are in love with theology are wounded, tired, and dry because they have theologically blocked off the wine of heaven."

"My hunger is for my future experience of Jesus; my satisfaction is my present experience; and my inspiration is my past experience of Him."

"Without humility a man has only the appearance of virtues."
—*Curé d'Ars*

"Jesus Christ is the best book; read Him."
—*Madame Guyon*

"God conceals the fullness of His speaking because our search for its fullness conditions the soul to contain it."

"You cannot separate fruitfulness and pleasure any more than you can get pregnant without an intimate, pleasurable experience."

"The highest efforts of mankind could never reach the miracle of the life of God in the soul of man."
—*Martyn Lloyd-Jones*

"You don't care what other people think when
you have seen Jesus as He really is."
—*Rodney Howard-Browne*

"Don't tell me you had an encounter with the Holy Spirit
and you don't cast out devils and heal the sick."
—*Rodney Howard-Browne*

"Learn humility. You can't fight Satan with Satan."
—*St. Padre Pio*

"The reason why so many people avoid silence in prayer
is because nothing so exposes hollowness as silence."

"The Bible is like prescription eyeglasses.
It is not vision, but through it you see clearly."

"Every time I find Him, He is resting. And when I join
Him there, His finished works become my reality."

"Faith is preferring spiritual and eternal realities
to the things of time."
—*Adolph Saphir*

"Hebrews is one continued and sustained, fervent, and
intense appeal to cleave to Jesus."
—*Adolph Saphir*

"You cannot separate a relationship with Jesus
and the experience of Jesus any more than you can
reduce your marriage to a photo."

"If you take experience out of a relationship,
all you have left is a memory."

"Be careful not to love preaching more
than you love people."
—*Fabian Grech*

"We don't endure Christianity; we enjoy Christianity."
—*Reinhard Bonnke*

"Our bodies are the locus (location)
of God's own presence."
—*Gordon Fee* (parentheses added)

"Before you judge someone, ask yourself this question:
'Who am I?'"
—*Monk Motto*

"Do not become anxious, because when you are
anxious, you cannot hear Me."
—*The Holy Spirit to Randy Clark*

Jonathan Edwards' wife, filled with the Spirit, was
drunk for seventeen days straight. Her revelation was of
"His nearness to me and my dearness to Him."

"Ministry is not the purpose of God touching your heart
with His presence—but it is the inevitable result. He
touches you because He loves you."

"Take experience out of relationship
and all that is left is an idea."

"Our relationship with the Spirit is no less experiential
than our initial encounter with Him."

"Religion is when we try to accomplish what can only
be accomplished by the Spirit."
—*Jack Deere*

"Backsliding is when your insides stop aching
for His presence."

"Every part of me that is not relaxed and at rest
in trust and surrender is working against
the sensible presence of God."

"If you feel called into ministry, then be willing to
disappear till God raises you up."
—*Dr. Jeff Hubing*

"If we are against living by a daily experience of God,
we indirectly believe the power of resolve is greater
than His empowering presence."

"Ministry must be our offspring instead of our mistress,
everything out of the union of intimacy."

"The two things that move heaven
are prayer and fasting."
—*David Hogan*

"To suggest, theologically or otherwise, a Christlikeness
without the need of His presence,
is blatant arrogance and self-confidence."

"You must pay a price to develop what is freely yours."
—*Bill Johnson*

Concerning miracles: "Have you been in His presence
and seen who He is, or have you learned who He is
and are manifesting that?"
—*Dan Mohler*

"Just like rainbows, you can only see the promises
of God in the light of day."

"Whatever doesn't issue from waiting upon God,
from depending upon the Holy Spirit,
is unquestionably of the flesh."
—*Watchman Nee*

"He who cleaves to me in trust and dependence
will continuously, from his innermost being,
have a flowing river of living water."
—*Jesus* (John 7:38; my paraphrase)

"New converts are automatic evangelists
because of an encounter. Continuous encounters
keep evangelism automatic."

"The experience of God doesn't come from the detachment from all things, but rather causes the detachment from all things."

"If we have the Spirit just like Jesus did, then what is the difference between us and His earthly life? The way He thought."
—*Dr. Robert Gladstone*

"The only way for this to be 'Your Best Life Now' is if you are going to hell."
—*John MacArthur*

"What's amazing to me about a man like You— is that You raise the dead and You suffer too."
—*Jason Upton on Jesus*

"Attention worship leaders—in your song selection, remember, we don't join the angels until we adore Him."

"Relying on God has to start all over every day, as if nothing has yet been done."
—*C. S. Lewis*

"He that receives the Son of God as the Son of God shall become a son of God."
—*Adolph Saphir*

"My soul suffers out of desire for Him."
—*St. Teresa of Jesus*

"Precious lamb of Calvary—
let thy Holy Spirit fall on me."
—*Barbara Stoddart*

"Illumination is inseparable from consecration."
—*See John 7:17*

"Many times our itch to be the one ministering
is evidence of the fact that we are not content
to be wholly His."

"People only bash the manifestations that
they don't see in their own lives."

"To all those who have much to say on revival—
have you ever seen it?"

"Most of the indelible imprints of His speaking
are unintelligible. He is more interested
in making us than informing us."

"...anyone who is serious about a prayer life
must...still the wanderings of the mind and the
restlessness of his heart."
—*St. Teresa of Jesus*

Concerning prayer, St. Teresa of Jesus says,
"He is only waiting for us to look at Him."

"The true spiritual life is being pulled into God,
by God, while still remaining yourself."
—*C. S. Lewis*

"How to stay hungry—don't eat anything but Jesus."

"All the struggles of a self-righteous soul are to put the
crown on your own head instead of at the feet of Jesus."
—*Robert Murray McCheyne*

"It is not a look into your own heart or the heart of hell,
but a look into the heart of Jesus that breaks the heart."
—*Robert Murray McCheyne*

"Impatience is disinterest in the Dove."

"The soul has a natural digression that if it is not
consciously turned to worship God, it will keep the
religious language and worship itself."

Someone once said, "
Tongues is the crackle of a heart on fire."

"We are most truly ourselves when we lose ourselves."
—*Thomas Merton*

"The sweet inebriation of His presence numbs
the faculty of reason with which we question
faith, trust, and surrender."

"After the millions have been saved
and healed and I sit on my bed at night,
it is still only God Himself that satisfies."
—*Daniel Kolenda*

"The finished work of the cross is finished—but that
finished work is not finished working on you."
—*Jeremy Johnson*

"Christ was made a puppet for men
who played the fool."
—*C. H. Spurgeon*

"The more vile Christ hath made Himself for us,
the more dear He ought to be to us."
—*St. Bernard of Clairvaux*

"Jesus is still mocked today—
for men mock the Master in the servant."
—*C. H. Spurgeon*

"The reason why congregations have been so dead
is because dead men preach to them."
—*George Whitefield*

"These sufferings are not hell because
He gives them the grace of His presence.
Hell is to be without His presence."
—*Richard Wurmbrand*

"Lord, protect me from living without listening."

"It is our liberty (to choose) that makes us persons, created in the image of God."
—*Thomas Merton*

"God is not responsible for an inconsistent experience of His presence."

"The garment of religion is a straitjacket."

"In prayer—delight is found just after the itch to move on dies."

"Religion is trying to access God through a door that doesn't exist."
—*Andrew Lamb*

"You could take a bath in a pool of wine, but until you drink it, you won't feel it burn in your chest."

"Lack of joy is rooted in ignorance of Christ's victories."

"His people delight in His will to the degree that they delight in Him. The service of the Lord is the joy of him whose joy is the Lord."

"Hell is to be outside the will of God."
—*David Popovici*

"In between the fullness of the Spirit and the power of the Spirit is an identity test."
—*See Luke 4*

"If we don't withdraw with Him,
we withdraw from Him."

"What is revival but the Reviver amongst us?"
—*David Popovici*

"It is good to love life, but sin to love your own life."
—*Dr. Michael L. Brown*

"An unsatisfied heart is an idol factory."

"Our only business (occupation or responsibility)
is to love and delight ourselves in God."
—*Brother Lawrence*

"Religion is trying to teach people to live according
to principles of a nature they do not possess."
—*David Popovici*

"We don't become like Jesus to experience the presence.
We experience the presence to become like Jesus."
—*David Popovici*

"Seeing Jesus alive in him changed my life."
—*Danielle Popovici on the life of her husband,
David Popovici*

"Lord, help me to never let the presence of another
person eclipse the presence of Your Spirit."

"When His sufferings eclipse your sufferings,
you are becoming invincible."
—*Michael Koulianos*

"The joy of the Lord preaches without preaching."
—*Mother Teresa*

"What signs, wonders, and miracles are saying
is that Jesus Christ has raised from the dead."
—*David Popovici*

"His blood is a portal."
—*Brian Guerin*

"Judas heard all Christ's sermons."
—*Thomas Goodwin*

"God, deliver me from the lust of always having
to vindicate myself."
—*St. Augustine*

"God can cure ignorance,
but for insincerity there is no cure."
—*A. W. Tozer*

"An ounce of trust is worth more than a ton of prayer."

"A fragrant aroma to God is not a song
but a crushed will."

"You want God to come in? God will come in in the
measure in which you go out."
—*T. Austin-Sparks*

"Only if your kingdom is 'of this world'
will you defend yourself."

"When Tommy Tenney came to preach, everyone
was so hungry at the altar. But when 5 a.m. came
the next morning, everyone was sleeping."
—*Journal entry 10.04.1999 in the dorms*

"It is only hard work when we do it
without the Holy Spirit."
—*Kathryn Kuhlman*

"Lust is the craving for salt in the man dying of thirst."
—*St. Augustine*

"Do you see a man who is arrogant?
The kingdom is not his."
—*Journal, 2004*

"Holy silence is when the presence of God expels all
sound entering the soul into His voice."

"The thing God saw most fit to make His church
bear the image of Christ in the book of Acts
was the wine of His Spirit."

"When God thus encounters no resistance, He does His own will in the soul, drawing it to and into Himself."
—*John Tauler, The Illuminated Doctor*

"In silence and solitude, the illusion that we can live separate from God is shattered."
—*Thomas Merton*

"A book on advanced prayer is a book on advanced joy."
—*Father Thomas Dubay, S.M.*

"Mary of Bethany scandalizes every man who loves the work of the Lord more than the Lord of the work."

"Where I pray is irrelevant, because once I begin to pray, I am not where I am anyway."

"Anyone who sees himself in the mirror and believes he has gone a day without sin, needs a brighter light in the room."

"Wherever reason is prevalent, revelation is not."
—*Tony Kemp*

"Faith is a result of revelation."
—*Tony Kemp*

"The cross is the end of self-consciousness."
—*Tony Kemp*

"To hurry God is to find fault with Him."
—*Walter Buetler*

"The glory of the Lord is the manifestation
of the person of Jesus Christ through the undeniable
presence of the Spirit."

"Under the influence of the Spirit it is impossible
to be influenced by others."

"I would rather move Him than understand Him."
—*Martha Kilpatrick*

"The evangelist is possessed with the desire to bring
the reward of Christ's sufferings to Him."
—*David Popovici*

"Bible study without Bible experience is pointless."
—*Bill Johnson*

"The soul is not a source, but that which is animated
by the source. Like filament in a bulb,
it is dependent on electricity for illumination."

"People tend to give more attention to the shooting star
than to the One that has burned steady and
constant for thousands of years."
—*David Popovici*

"The cost of discipleship isn't nearly as expensive
as the cost of nondiscipleship."
—*David Popovici*

"The Holy Spirit's resting place is in the resting soul."

"If the devil can get you restless,
he has you at his mercy."

"The proof of having been apprehended by God
is seeking to apprehend God."

"True prayer is coming to Jesus
and finding rest for your soul."
Tongues vs. Silence

"I can hear the sound of the waves
Breaking upon the shore.
But as I proceeded to the depths,
I could hear them no more."

"Seek with great diligence in prayer that you may come
to a spiritual feeling or sight of God."
—*Walter Hilton*

"Abiding in Christ is the continuous extraction
of ecstatic rapturous delight from God
through Christ by the Spirit."

"Whatever doesn't issue out of divine
interaction is an entanglement."

"James says the words, 'greater grace,'
which tells me there is a way into more grace
than what I currently am empowered by."

"Men must turn to God from the earth
in order to taste of God's sweetness."
—*Richard Rolle*

"My soul yearns deeply; suffers with longing; longs
painfully; is homesick for the presence of God."
—*Psalm 84:2, AMP*

"Your fruit is found in Me."
—*Hosea 14:9, ONM*

"The difficulty of the spiritual life is in exact proportion
to the attention you give to the self-life."

"The negative side to the intimacy movement is that
many have only adopted the language."

"Operation in the new nature necessitates
recognition of the old nature."

"Giving God my life means preaching the Gospel."
—*Fabian Grech*

"Covenant is stewarding and advancing the call of God
on your brother's life and family."
—*David Popovici*

"Neglecting time with God is the most
dangerous thing you can do."
—*Benny Hinn*

"Communion with Christ is a certain cure for every ill."
—*Charles Spurgeon*

"You cannot reflect a brighter light than what you
yourself have actually seen."

"Until the spirit of harlotry has no place in you,
you cannot take dominion over her."

"You must behold His glory to be transformed
into His likeness."

"Purity consists in clinging with passionate
desire to God alone."
—*John Ruusbroec*

"All things are to be used by us,
but God is to be enjoyed."
—*John Ruusbroec*

"I have plenty of talents at my disposal. What I desire
is for a soul to make it my place of rest."
—*Jesus to Mary of the Holy Trinity*

"Jesus is kind. Do not misrepresent Him."
—*Sr. Consolata Betrone*

"God resists the resistant."
—*Daniel Kolenda*

"When God kisses someone,
the fragrance never goes away."
—*Daniel Kolenda*

Louis Borjon, a close friend of the Curé d'Ars, said of him, "I never saw a truer picture of the Divine Master."

"Sin makes stillness impossible."

"Glory is the tangible substance of God's person."

"Difficulty in spending time waiting in His presence comes from motives other than simply being with Him."

"Children are a result of intimacy, not the purpose."

"The sinner hates God because God i
s opposed to His selfishness."
—*Charles G. Finney*

"If we remove repentance from the Christian life, we destroy the bridge back to our first love."

"To not be still is to not allow Him to be King."

"Hyper-grace is obliterated by
the judgment seat of Christ."

"Mr. Performance, Frustration, and Competition
are the assassins of enjoying God."

"Some of us have strayed so far from our first love
that we don't remember what it is like."
—*Dr. Michael L. Brown*

"Some men describe honey; Jesus dispenses it."

"Self-righteousness is unrighteousness."
—*Jeremy Johnson*

"God never merely instructs. Through His speaking
to us, He enters us, uniting with our person,
fulfilling the thing by His own power."

"Some think because we are busy our attention to God
will suffer in some way. But they fail to realize that the
soul was made to do all things through staring at Jesus."

"You cannot complain and listen to God simultaneously."
—*See Psalm 106:25*

"We've become so positional that
it is no longer personal."
—*Dr. Jeff Hubing*

"The enemy of longevity is lopsided doctrine."

"Worship is the positioning; the word is
the receiving and prayer is the settling."

"As I look back over my life, it seems certain people
were there at different times to see whether
or not I could overcome their influence."

"Nothing destroys the love of the world
more than the bliss of Jesus."

"Nothing plagues the spiritual life more than
the soul's desire to work something up."

"When joy is no longer in the service,
the service is no longer unto the Lord."

"We receive the Word of God through the Scriptures."

"Worthless works issue out of restless souls."

"In worship, words are like oxygen. The higher you
ascend, the more absent they are."

"To see Him is to be united with Him."
—*Madame Guyon*

"Activity obstructs union."
—*Madame Guyon*

"Adoration is the purest form of seeking God."

"Clinging to the Lord is the refusal
to depart from His presence."

"The prophet constantly gives himself to
the passivity of listening, knowing that all he
is depends upon the reception of the word."

"The only way to bring heaven into earth
is to first live there yourself."

"Spiritual adultery is to look for satisfaction in another."
—See Hosea 2:7

"The Christian life is a paradoxical fusion
of attainment and yearning."

"If we do not abide in Him, we will soon find ourselves
in shame, bareness, and dissatisfaction."
—See Hosea 2:4, 5

"Why should I stand up here and try to be something
when You became nothing?"
—Heidi Baker

"Repentance isn't a one-time decision to look to Jesus as
much as it is a decision to always decide look to Jesus."

"To love Jesus is to love what He taught."

"One day you are going to want mercy, so you better
give it to everyone, every chance you get."

"Within grace are all the things necessary
for sanctification."
—*Madame Guyon*

"Religion is presenceless devotion."

"Contemplation is only possible in and
through the Scriptures."
—*Gregory the Great*

"He dwells where He reigns and He reigns
where He dwells."
—*See Psalm 68:16*

"The reason why worry is a sin is because
it is impossible to worry when our attention
is turned toward His presence."

"Solitude is the furnace of transformation."
—*Henri Nouwen*

"Christ is a person, and when He is yielded to,
He becomes a state of being."

"Solitude removes outward distractions, silence
removes inward distractions, and prayer centers the
heart on God—here He is found with ease."

"There doesn't exist a greater fusion of joy and sorrow
than at the Lord's table."

"Ceaseless prayer is a heart consciously
fixed upon God as it weaves in and out,
passing through all of life's obstacles."

"Waiting is refusing to move on, settling in the bliss
of adoration, with absolutely no other agenda,
until His face lights up the next step."

"Sin is not bearing God's image correctly."
—*Jeff Hubing*

"If any man thinks ill of you, do not be angry with him,
for you are worse than he thinks you to be."
—*Charles Spurgeon*

"One moment in ecstasy in God's presence
is more valuable than twenty years of
exhaustive intellectual effort."
—*St. Teresa of Avila*

"Lucifer was perfect. Pride was enough
for God to disapprove him."

"To walk in the Spirit is to shatter all passions
with the pleasure of His presence."

"Waiting on the Lord is impossible for a soul whose
attention, desire, and intentions are divided."

"Listening, watching, and waiting are dispositions
of a soul whose desire is exclusively for Him."

"The seductive spirit offers delight
without commitment."
—*See Proverbs 7:18*

"Secret—in the place of solitude and adoration,
the itch to do something stems from wanting
something more or other than just Him."

"At first I sought to whip men into the image of Christ;
now I seek to woo men into Christ's image."

"The false prophets were rebuked for superficially
treating the fracture of God's people; like putting
a Band-Aid on a broken arm."
—*See Jeremiah 6:14*

"The anointing will wow you,
but only the Glory will woo you."

"The anointing will set a man free from bondage and
sickness, but only the glory will overtake a man's heart."

"If beholding His glory transforms us into His likeness,
then not beholding His glory would cause
us to remain in our own likeness."

"When we know Him as all,
all our problems are solved. I therefore have no other
message than this: Christ is all."
—*Watchman Nee*

"I speak those things I have seen
in the presence of my Father."
—*Jesus, John 8:38; Sons speak out what they've seen
in the presence.*

"'If you continue in My word, then you are truly
My disciple.' To deny obedience to Christ's words
is to no longer follow Him."

"The ease of your secret place depends
upon the strength of your abiding place; and the
strength of your abiding place depends upon
the strength of your secret place."

"The root of our new life is not merely a daily
realization but rather a daily renunciation."

"Worship is not some performance we do,
but a presence we experience."
—*A. W. Tozer*

"I accomplish more when I rest wholly
in the labor of Jesus than I do when I frantically
try to do the work for Him."
—*A. W. Tozer*

"A personal relationship with God is a continuous,
never-ending and constantly increasing
experience of Him."

"Trying to be happy without a sense of God's presence
is like trying to have a bright day without the sun."
—*A. W. Tozer*

"Stillness into adoration will tear the soul
away from the influence of the body and pass it
into the dominion of the Spirit."

"You will have a implacable hatred toward sin
when you look upon it as the executioner of Jesus."
—*St. Gerard Majella*

"Faith is my life, and life, for me, is faith."
—*St. Gerard Majella*

"I will never accuse others, nor speak
of their defects, not even in jest."
—*St. Gerard Majella*

"The deviated gaze results in devious speech."
—*See Proverbs 4:24-25*

"Honesty is more inspiring than exaggeration."

"The life which lives near to God,
from its very nature...can receive far more than
the active souls of heavenly mysteries."
—*Andrew Jukes*

"There is no service like unconscious service,
which naturally flows from what we are through
the divine indwelling."
—*Andrew Jukes*

"That man is a copy of the living Christ."
—*Said of Gerard Majella*

"The will of God! The will of God! O, how happy is he
who knows how to will the will of God!"
—*St. Gerard Majella*

"I am in the wounds of Jesus Christ
and His wounds are in me."
—*St. Gerard Majella*

"The presence doesn't remove the storm;
it takes you out from under its influence."

"The desire to be recognized is to not recognize Jesus."

"If Christ is not life, we have to do the work;
but if HE is life, we need not struggle."
—*Watchman Nee*

"A reward is earned; Jesus is a gift."

"God creates out of nothing. Therefore, until a man is
nothing, God can make nothing out of him."
—*Martin Luther*

"Every spiritual thing outside of Christ is dead."
—*Watchman Nee*

"Why do I read the Bible so much?
Because I am addicted to the electric sensation
of the voice of the Spirit."

"It is immaturity to think that God's love
for us is dependent upon what we do; but it is
equally immature to think His pleasure isn't."

"My heart is breaking with joy."

"Bondage is when the devil has sown himself into the
will of man by passing on to man his thinking patterns."

"You become a voice by listening to His voice."

"Nothing will put out the fire of
sinful desires like the rain of His presence."

"One of the most incredible works
of the glory is childlikeness."

"Manipulation can bear some fruit;
obligation will appear to bear the most fruit;
but only love will bear significant fruit."

"What we do in time of failure is the same as what we
do in success...come to Jesus."

"He manifests His glory, to us, through us, and in us."

"The first time Jesus used the word 'church'
about His followers is when they used the word
'Messiah/King' about Him."
—*Dr. Robert Gladstone*

"Jesus without experience is just fact.
Jesus with experience is The Truth."
—*Andrew Lamb*

"Adoration is clinging to His presence.

Self-consciousness is withdrawal from His presence."

"If I lose sight of my imperfection,
I find it necessary to magnify what a fellow
imperfect person has done wrong."

"My imperfection demands that I magnify the things
a fellow imperfect person has done right
and not what they have done wrong."

"I ask You to untie us from the bonds of all our sins,
as You allowed Yourself to be tied up for love of us."
—*Richard Rolle*

"We are only a light if we are in the Light."

"Feelings are always present.
We are never not feeling something."
—*Philip Krill,* Life in the Trinity

"We don't wait *for* His presence;
we wait *in* His presence."

"The valley of the shadow of death is not
when the presence has left you but when
the presence is all that you have left."

"Prayer is the source of illumination and is
a part of every stage of growth."
—*Angela of Foligno*

"The sense of His presence is the indication that
we are drawing from the source of Life Himself."

"You can take the church, you can take my Bible
and my clothes, but you can't take His presence."
—*Leonard Ravenhill*

"The holy life is tasting His divine sweetness
and losing taste for everything else."

"Both the Scriptures and mystical experience flow from
the same wellspring in God's life,
and mutually enlighten one another."
—*Angela of Foligno*

"A Gospel without repentance is demonic."
—*Benny Hinn*

"Psalm 86:14 shows us that arrogance comes
from a lack of His presence."

"Divine ease is only a reality in the life that is
exclusively yoked to Jesus."

"You're not with me because I am holy.
You're with me to make me holy."

"The busyness of things obscures our concentration on
God. We must maintain a position of beholding Him."
—*Oswald Chambers*

"When we truly see Him, we never say, 'I am holy.'
We say, 'He is holy.' Even after we are glorified,
that will be the case."

"What is abiding? A conscious yielding in adoration into
a continuous, sensible experience of the Spirit
that produces effortless holy living."

"Staleness is an indication that something
in our lives is out of step with God."
—*Oswald Chambers*

"A test is not to see how good you can do
on your own, but rather to see if you will continue
to abide in His presence."

"If God had to leave you to test you,
that would mean that He is trying to fashion you
into something apart from Himself."

"Lord, make me simple enough to believe Your Word."
—*Mel Tari*

"The secret to becoming like Him is only wanting Him."

"In the womb God reduced Himself to a fetus;
in the manger, an infant; but on the cross, a worm.
No one could possibly love us like this."

"Conviction is God offering you the gift of repentance."

"The deepest communion with God is when our
adoration becomes wordless and the soul is suspended
in a glorious exchange of life for life."

"The soul will become so still in adoration that
it will settle completely content upon the wholeness
of the Spirit—raptured in delight."

"Joy is the evidence of divine enablement."
—*See Psalm 21:1*

"The honeymoon period doesn't have
to come to an end."
—*Peter Madden*

"Here is the rule for everyday life: Do not do anything that you cannot offer to God."
—*Curé d'Ars*

"Paul didn't get locked up for two years because he told Felix he was amazing and that God loved him."

•

•

NOTES

NOTES

NOTES

NOTES

NOTES

NOTES

NOTES

NOTES

NOTES

NOTES

NOTES

ABOUT THE AUTHOR

I met Jesus the first day that I saw Evangelist Steve Hill at Brownsville Assembly of God in Pensacola, Florida, in 1996. His face was radiating with light, and for the first time in my life, Jesus was manifested to me in the preaching of the cross in the power of the Spirit. I have not been the same since.

I graduated the Brownsville Revival School of Ministry in 2001, then returned to FIRE school of ministry to enter Dr. Michael L. Brown's mentoring group in 2002. In 2003 I started working at Christ for all Nations, the ministry of Reinhard Bonnke. I was married in 2004 to the love of my life. Today we have two girls, Madison and Lia. In the summer of 2010 God spoke to my heart said, "I want you to be my spokesman." After a two weeks' notice, I quit working construction and started giving my life to the Gospel alone. Since that day, God has been gracious to back His Gospel with signs, wonders, and miracles. Cancers, hepatitis, broken bones, and many more sicknesses have been crushed by the name of Jesus. Hundreds have surrendered their lives to Jesus in response to the Gospel. We are under a mandate from the Lord to set the captives free by the power of the Spirit. But the center of our hearts in God is to bring about a deeper awareness, consciousness, and experience of God's presence in the lives of every believer.

Those that are led by the Spirit are the sons of God. SONSHIP!

Eric William Gilmour
sonship-international.org
eric@sonship-international.org

NEW BOOK! Order Here.

God is raising up mystical wonder workers who seek oneness with God through surrender and bleed deliverance to this sin-sick world. These are the Jesus people, possessed by God and manifesting Him in character, power, and wisdom. In this

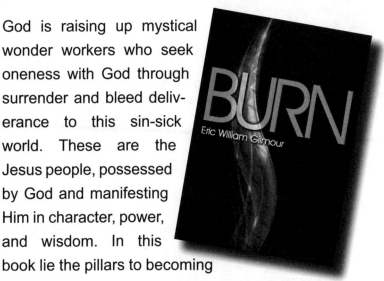

book lie the pillars to becoming the Jesus people. This book will be a manual to fuel the revolution of those who bear Christ's image in the earth. May God consume your life and swallow up everything contrary to Him with the glorious pleasure of Himself.

Price: $10.99 (ISBN-978-0-615-64343-4)

Available at:
Amazon.com
BarnesandNoble.com
http://sonship-international.org/
order-burn-melting-into-the-image-of-jesus/